Routledge Library Editions

THE CHIMBU

ANTHROPOLOGY AND ETHNOGRAPHY

Routledge Library Editions
Anthropology and Ethnography

SOUTH PACIFIC AND AUSTRALASIA
In 9 Volumes

I	The Great Village	*Belshaw*
II	Under the Ivi Tree	*Belshaw*
III	The Chimbu	*Brown*
IV	Mambu	*Burridge*
V	Sorcerers of Dobu	*Fortune*
VI	Migrations, Myth and Magic from the Gilbert Islands	*Grimble*
VII	A Diary in the Strict Sense of the Term	*Malinowski*
VIII	Rautahi	*Metge*
IX	Coming into Being among the Australian Aborigines	*Montagu*

THE CHIMBU

A Study of Change in the New Guinea Highlands

PAULA BROWN

R Routledge
Taylor & Francis Group
LONDON AND NEW YORK

First published in 1973

Reprinted in 2004 by
Routledge
2 Park Square, Milton Park, Abingdon, Oxfordshire OX14 4RN

Transferred to Digital Printing 2009

Routledge is an imprint of the Taylor & Francis Group

First issued in paperback 2013

British Library Cataloguing in Publication Data
A CIP catalogue record for this book is available from the British Library

ISBN: 978-0-415-86663-7

Miniset: South Pacific and Australasia

Series: Routledge Library Editions – Anthropology and Ethnography

The Chimbu
A Study of Change in the
New Guinea Highlands

Paula Brown

Routledge & Kegan Paul
London

First published in Great Britain in 1973 by
Routledge & Kegan Paul Ltd
Broadway House, 68–74 Carter Lane
London EC4V 5EL

Printed in Great Britain
by Unwin Brothers Limited
The Gresham Press, Old Woking, Surrey, England
A member of the Staples Printing Group

You and the Native was originally published in February 1943 for the Allied Geographical Section, the Southwest Pacific area. It is reproduced here in its entirety.

ISBN 0 7100 7572 3

Contents

Foreword by J. A. Barnes		vii
Map of New Guinea		x
Map of the Chimbu		xi
1.	Introduction	1
2.	The Chimbu View of Past and Future	5
3.	The Kinds of Variation and Change	9
4.	Chimbu Pre-History	14
5.	Chimbu's First Contact with Europeans	23
6.	Domestic and Local Groups	29
7.	Groups and Segments	35
8.	Big Men and Small	41
9.	Cycles and Transactions	45
10.	Strife	51
11.	Warfare	57
12.	The Process of Change	65
13.	The Forces of Change	69
14.	Material and Technological Change	78
15.	Economic Change	86
16.	Local Leadership and Activities	93
17.	Conflict Today	101
18.	Kondom's Kingdom	110
19.	Plus ça change, plus c'est la même chose	121
	Appendix I. Glossary	127
	Appendix II. You and the Native	129
	References	145
	Index	149

List of Tables

I. Some Causes of Warfare in Chimbu 62

II. Composition of Marriage Payments in
Central Chimbu 1958-65 91

III. Dispute Cases Discussed in Court with Native Leaders 104

IV. Cases Taken from Local Discussion to Government
Office for Hearing 106

V. Cases in Court of Native Affairs and
Native Matters, 1959-60 107

Foreword

by J. A. BARNES

THIS BOOK should need no introduction from me. Paula Brown and the Chimbu people whose social life she discusses are both already well-known to wide audiences. In association with Harold Brookfield, Dr. Brown has presented students with the Chimbu as a most interesting example of the many peoples who have had to make, in the course of a few decades, a radical change from the relative insulation of a Stone Age culture to the progressive turbulence of the modern world. The Chimbu themselves have proclaimed their identity as one of the most vigorous and energetic groups in New Guinea, determined to play a prominent part in the political and economic development of their country.

The level of technical attainment reached by the Chimbu in 1933 corresponded to that found in Europe several millennia ago at the end of the New Stone Age. Politically, the Chimbu corresponded approximately to the tribes who inhabited northern Europe before the rise of the Roman Empire. Chimbu District still does not look like Europe (I hope it never will), but it now uses the same alphabet, part of the same technology, some of the same symbols and, most importantly, the same system of world-wide markets and prices. It is easy to be deceived by these similarities and to think that they are the result of an enormously accelerated version of a process of change which in Europe took centuries to run its course.

Dr. Brown explains what really happened. The Chimbu have traveled at a different speed but also along a different road. The process whereby Chimbu tribesmen may appear to have become Chimbu peasants has provided them with some of the outward forms of Western civilization but its speed has left them free to adopt, and indeed has forced them to invent, their own interpretation of these forms. For the Chimbu, the future of literacy, or of seemingly Western forms of organization — councils, courts, monogamous marriage — is unlikely to follow traditional Western paths. Furthermore, this process of radical change has provided the Chimbu with only the products, and only some of the products, of Western technology without the full range of skills and of capital investment that lies behind them. Like many other so-called 'developing' peoples, the Chimbu use tools they cannot produce and can scarcely repair; they must sell their crops at prices they cannot control. Here they are not merely qualitatively different from Western peasants; they are in a fundamentally weaker position. The old order has been destroyed and they have not mastered the new. Many passages in Dr. Brown's book show that the Chimbu are aware of their weakness. The suggestion of boredom which lurks between one ceremonial exchange and the next seems to spring from a recognition of their plight. The rapidity with which the Chimbu have made the transition from the Stone Age gives them the possibility of adapting Western achievements to new ends, but they cannot grasp this possibility without adequate economic and intellectual resources.

We can gain some understanding of how Chimbu society is likely to develop only because we are here provided with a careful account of how it has in fact changed, step by step, during the last forty years. Far too often the study of social change is based on a comparison of snapshots, the scene as it was then compared with the scene as it is now, with little hard evidence to show how the transition came about. Sometimes this limitation cannot be avoided. In many parts of Africa and Eurasia there has been indirect contact for many hundreds of years between centers of literate civilization and non-literate groups living far away, so that the search for a zero-point for the study of change is futile. In other parts of the world, where similar contacts began to occur more recently, the only records of traditional social life at the moment of first impact were made by explorers and adventurers. In the case of New Guinea, however, the Australian invasion of the Highlands is so recent that trained ethnographers were often among the first to observe and record the onset of irreversible change. With the Chimbu there is a gap of twenty-five years between 1933, when Taylor and his companions crossed their territory, and 1958 when Paula Brown began her inquiries in the field. This gap is not as serious as it might seem, for there are useful records of the intervening period made by prospectors, missionaries and administrators. Dr. Brown was able to talk to many men and women who remembered the old days before the arrival of outsiders. She can match her findings against the evidence provided by ethnographers who have worked in other Highland societies since the end of the 1940's. From 1958 she has the results of her frequent visits to the field. Thus she can provide a firmly based account of how successive stages in the process of change were reached and passed.

Yet even before 1933 Chimbu society was never static. Professor Brown stresses that continual change was a permanent feature of the traditional political order. Indeed, much of the difficulty still encountered in the settlement of Chimbu land disputes stems from the false assumption that the spatial disposition of groups at the moment when Australian administrative control was first imposed represented a traditional configuration.

In fact, boundaries were continually changing and political alliances continually being formed and broken. Yet despite incidents such as the introduction of the sweet potato, and despite a gradual increase in the density of population, there may well have been consistency and continuity in the traditional forms of conflict, and in the value system embedded in Chimbu culture. A repetitive model may fit traditional Chimbu society but after 1933 there have been changes of quality as well as of quantity, so that the model must be modified to allow for irreversible and cumulative change.

Fortunately the fluidity of their social life seems to have enabled the Chimbu to face the uncertainties of the present with a readiness to experiment and innovate which should stand them in good stead. They find themselves now on the threshold of freshly perplexing changes as the colonial phase moves to its end. Paula Brown has provided a most stimulating account of the Chimbu at a critical point in their history.

Churchill College
Cambridge University

J. A. Barnes
Professor of Sociology

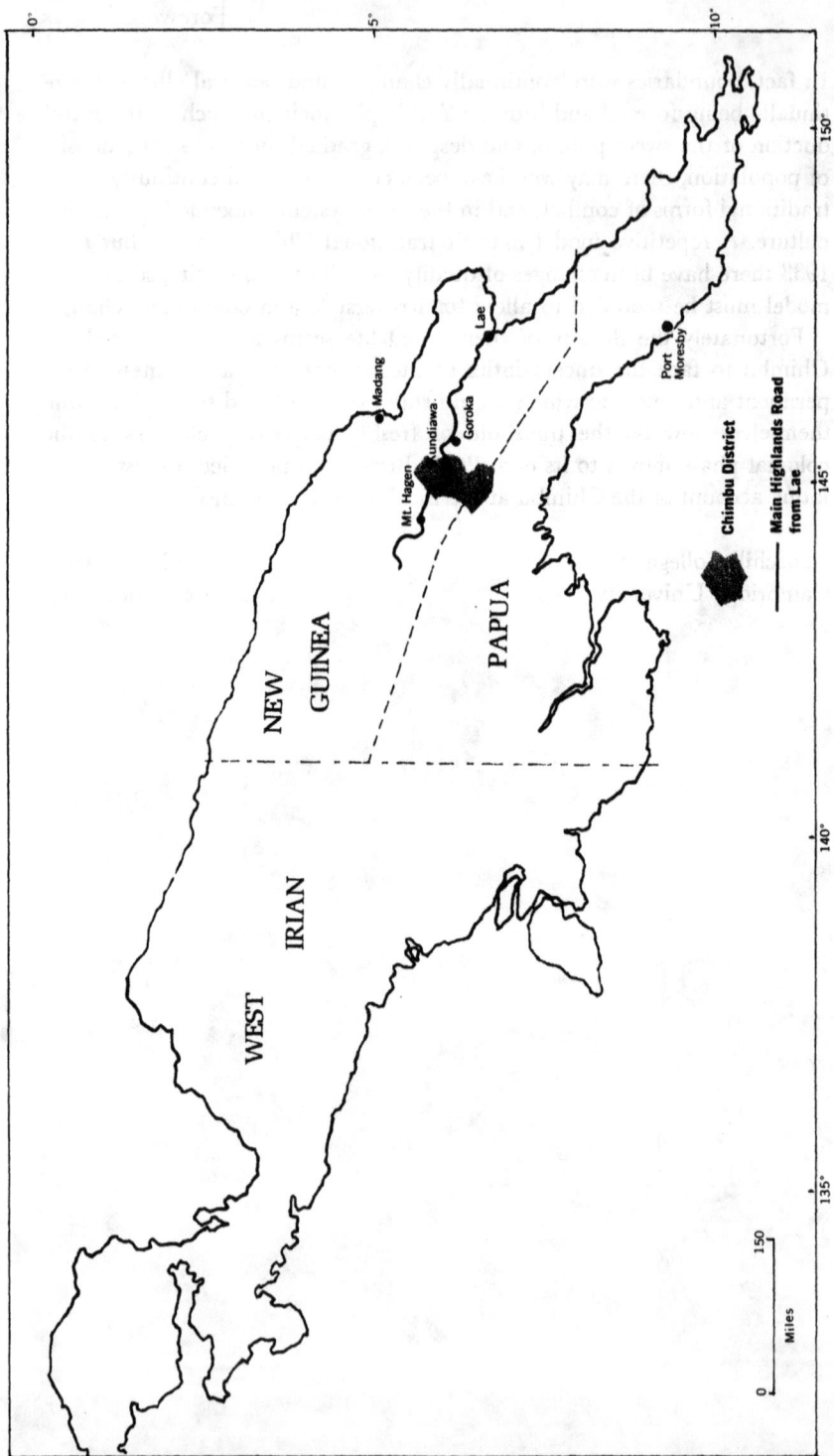

New Guinea

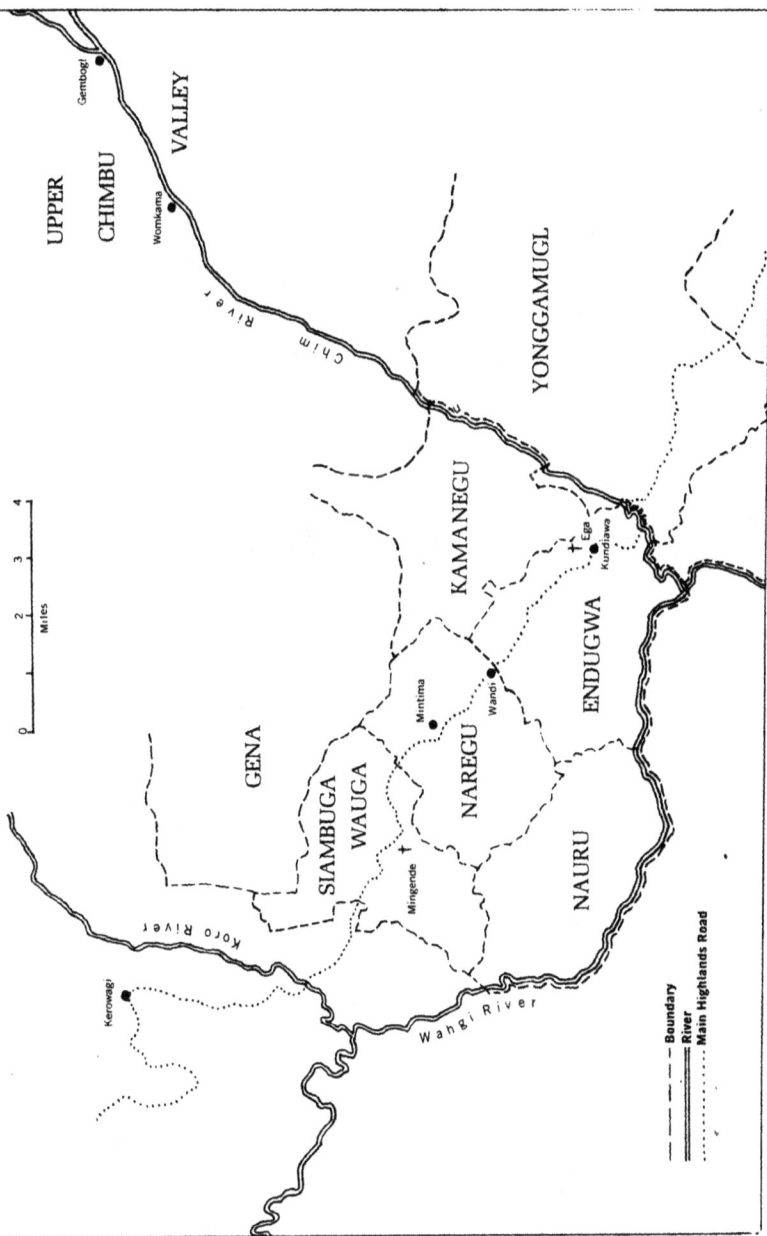

The Chimbu

To Ira, who pushed me into
it and pulled me through.

Chapter 1

Introduction

WHEN I FIRST planned to study the Chimbu, I chose them from among the New Guinea highlands people for the special characteristics which enable me to write this book. The discovery in the 1930's of the dense populations in the New Guinea highlands was an unparalleled opportunity to record the first phases of western contact and social change of isolated peoples. Anthropologists have always been interested in the situation of first contact and speculated about the reactions, interactions and events which occurred. Some record exists in many areas, but the questions modern anthropologists ask developed only after most of the world had some experience of the west. America, Africa and Asia were discovered and colonized by Europeans before anthropology became a recognized subject. The circumstances of first contact and subsequent events are, for the most part, lost. Thus the study of change among the New Guinea highland peoples is an exceptional opportunity for anthropologists.

Field conditions are never perfect for us to observe, record and explain the course of events. Still, for one interested as I am in social change, the Chimbu were almost ideal. They experienced none of the early and chance contacts of the coast, as they were far inland and surrounded by other highlands peoples. Their discovery by Australian prospectors was in the early 1930's,[1] and we have some record of the discovery and subsequent events. It was possible to interview some people present at early contact and throughout the period of contact. I had available some reports and

[1] No earlier explorations into the highlands reached Chimbu (Willis 1969).

1

observations of the Chimbu from 1933 onward. Of course, even under the best conditions of observation and recording, we can never claim a study as complete and fully accurate. But I do not think a better choice than Chimbu could have been made for a study of a generation of social change.

Chimbu are numerous and central in the highlands. They have spread out of the valley and are the densest and most populous group in New Guinea. The government post has been continuously at Kundiawa and mission posts at Ega, Mingende and in the Chimbu and Koro valleys since 1934 or 1935. There is then some record of them since discovery and some descriptions of their changing culture that already have been published (Nilles, Schaefer).

When I arrived in 1956, The Australian National University Department of Anthropology and Sociology, established by the late S. F. Nadel, had a plan to study New Guinea highlands ethnography and several studies had already been undertaken. Soon after I joined that department, a conference on New Guinea highlands studies was held in Canberra. The research already done indicated that New Guinea highlands societies were similar, yet significantly different from those known elsewhere. Further work was needed to explore their variations. My own entry into the field was due to W. E. H. Stanner's encouragement and when J. A. Barnes came to The Australian National University, he suggested that I try to follow one highland community through an important period of change. I decided to work in Chimbu in collaboration with H. C. Brookfield whose interests in population distribution, settlement and agriculture would combine well with mine in social, political and economic anthropology and social change. Together we chose the central Chimbu area, in those days still remote from political and economic development but near the highlands road. The Naregu tribe and Mintima were chosen as outside the immediate neighborhood of Kundiawa (then Chimbu Sub-district headquarters, now Chimbu District headquarters) and Mingende Catholic mission. Furthermore, I was especially interested in Kondom, the Naregu *luluai* and leader.

During 1958, 1959 and 1960 I became familiar with the society in general, and in collaboration with H. C. Brookfield studied land tenure and settlement. Thereafter visits of one to three months, mostly at Mintima, but also for days or weeks in other parts of Chimbu and Papua New Guinea, continued until I left The Australian National University late in 1965. Most recently, I visited there in August 1971.

Many residents of all races have given me hospitality and assistance and my work was greatly helped by members of the Papua New Guinea administration in Canberra, Port Moresby, Kundiawa and other parts of New Guinea. All of the field work and the data analysis, photographic processing and map drawing were supported by The Australian National

University. This included the building or repairing of several houses and maintaining them. In 1964 a house was built on land leased from some Mintima people and this has been used as a field station by a number of scholars since I left.

Since 1966 I have been at the State University of New York at Stony Brook. Summer fellowships, and research assistance as well as secretarial help provided by the University have facilitated the completion of this book. Other typing, map drawing and editing help has been generously given by the staff of Glick & Lorwin.

This work has been my main, if not sole, interest for almost fifteen years. It began and has continued through the stimulating interchange of facts and ideas with other scholars. The discussions have carried from New Guinea to Australia, England and the United States. In this time the New Guinea highlands has become the center of some important advances and controversies in social anthropological theory and in culture history.

This book is concerned with change among the Chimbu and is thus connected both with social anthropology and culture history. Social structure studies usually assume a persisting form of social grouping. But some of the problems of understanding New Guinea highlands social structure might be resolved if the societies were considered as constantly in flux rather than as fixed segmentary systems. Chimbu culture, groups and relations were constantly adapting to changing circumstances, but the long-term trends are not yet clear. Viewing the Chimbu as an adapting society is fundamental to understanding the changes which have been and are taking place now.

Our contemporary interest in changing societies of colonial and post-colonial periods is aimed at both general understanding and special problems. The accumulation of case studies is essential to arriving at generalizations and a theory of change. Each case study has some distinct or unique characteristics. In many places there is a lack of information on early contact and a long period of unrecorded colonialism preceding the present study. The New Guinea highlands is the last large area in the world where first contact is within living memory. All direct effects of colonial administration and other forces of westernization have been since 1933. Papua New Guinea is preparing for independence this decade. Thus the people of the New Guinea highlands may have the world's shortest colonial history. While this study does not carry the Chimbu into an era of general education, modern technology, economics or law, it describes the rapid early phases of westernization and social change.

This book falls naturally into three parts: the first introductory, theoretical and historical, chapters 1-5; the second concerning the dynamics of tribal life, chapers 6-11; and the third on aspects of change, chapters 12-19.

In writing this book, I have drawn upon some previously published works, and particularly from some of my own articles. Parts of the papers listed in the references as Brown 1967a, 1967b, 1970a and 1970b are taken with only minor changes into chapters 7, 8, 9, 14, 15 and 18. I am grateful to the editors of *Anthropological Forum*, the *Journal of the Papua and New Guinea Society*, *Man* and the *Southwestern Journal of Anthropology* for permission to do this. I also appreciate permission to quote from Vial's paper in *Walkabout*, 1938, and from Leahy and Crain, 1937, Funk and Wagnall's, New York.

A glossary of terms in the text is found in Appendix I.

Appendix II is from a handbook prepared apparently by an Australian author for the Allied Geographical Section, Southwest Pacific Area, 1943.

Chapter 2

The Chimbu View of Past and Future

MANY ANTHROPOLOGICAL studies assume or imply that, prior to discovery by western explorers, traders or missionaries, the native people of the non-western world had an unchanging way of life, engaging in stable pursuits — gathering wild plants and insects, weaving baskets, worshipping ancestors, exchanging sisters, avoiding mothers-in-law, or performing whatever cultural activities struck the first observer as noteworthy. I consider this view of traditional life both wrong and misleading — all people are constantly changing and adapting to new environmental and social circumstances.

The "clash of culture" formulation is another common misconception — the native peoples are portrayed as innocent and defenseless, forced to submit to western germs, wheels, evangelism and alcohol, from which they have suffered immeasurably. Demoralized and debilitated, they have been forced into twentieth-century materialism. Such a sentimental interpretation leads to pity, paternalism and the imagined possible return to the lost golden age. Such a view of past and present is false in many respects, as I hope my account of the Chimbu will make clear.

One important variable among peoples is their own view of their past. The Chimbu do not think that their way of life was stable and unchanging. Rather, they recount stories of fights, fleeing from victorious enemies, expansion movements, migrations, inventions, and see their lives as forever in change and flux.

Despite persistent questioning, I could not elicit from any Chimbu certain sorts of traditions common elsewhere. They have no systematic cosmological beliefs. Nor had they stories describing, or even implying, a

5

fixed order of the natural world. There are stories about how things began which concern human characteristics, cultural practices or objects such as gardening, pigs, cooking, sexual intercourse, and intertribal relations. This is in striking contrast with the Australian aborigines, whose interests and beliefs concentrate upon the idea of everlasting time, an eternal "dream-time," continuous with the present in which the ancestors live (Stanner 1956). Chimbus, unlike many peoples in change, do not look upon the past as a lost golden age. Nor do they see their history and tradition as an irreversible movement from the primitive past to the progressive future. No such definite trend is recognized. It is rather as though they feel that the world is always changing and unpredictable.

These aspects of their world view are well exemplified in Chimbu language forms. Simplicity of tense is complemented by a large number of special modal forms, with factual, negative, intensive, relative, uncertain and dubitative forms. They distinguish by verb forms that which they know from that which may be in doubt. They have only numerals one and two — anything more is by duplication and "many." Nor have they measures for time by minutes or years.

It is worth studying the people's conception of their past and the stability or instability of their lives, their history, their traditions, their interest in time, dates or ages or seniority. These interests and attitudes help the anthropologist to understand the people, on the basis of their beliefs, their attitude towards continuity or change, their desire for something new, or their valuing of the old days, the esteem that they give to conservative or changing leaders. We can find in people anywhere propensities to change and not to change. In many societies, conservatives are distinguished from progressives, elders from youths, the privileged from the emerging. There are commonly conflicting individuals or factions; in an institutionalized political system, these become political parties with conflicting policies or election issues.

We can also see how a society values its cultural origins, beliefs and customs. For example, once when I was visiting A. L. and T. S. Epstein in the Tolai area, we spoke to a Tolai leader about the continued use of *tambu* shell money although most cash transactions were in Australian currency. He said, "If we didn't have *tambu* we wouldn't be Tolai." (See A. L. Epstein 1969: 317.)

Clinging to symbols, honoring past heroes, etc., are all signs of the continued importance of tradition. In Chimbu, the past is not honored, the aged are ridiculed. One day, when I attempted to inquire of an elderly Chimbu about the conditions of his youth and young adulthood, before and early in the days of European contact, his adult son said to me, "He's an old man and he doesn't know anything; what are you talking to him

for?" When a land claim case was being considered by a Lands Commissioner, a group came together to discuss their claims and called on the
old men to recall evidence to support their claims to the land. But the old
men were obviously uncomfortable at being placed in this position: they
had not been consulted or heard for years, and recognized the artificiality
of the situation. These tales of yore were collected for the Lands Commissioner's benefit; Chimbu men would much rather fight for the control of
land.

Chimbu concern for the present is indicated in the patterns of social
relations and the absence of genealogical recall. Ties are more common
with affines than with kin, and adopted members are not distinguished
from birth members of groups. Periodic ceremonies in Chimbu affirm
present ties. There are no ever-enduring clan and tribe ties; there are not
exclusive lineal connections even in Womkama, regarded by all Chimbu as
the source and place of origin (Criper 1967). Tribes are made up of local
alliances, and migrating groups form new alliances. Further, the Chimbu
use of kinship terms reflects current relations, not genealogical ties. A boy
may call his older brother 'father' because this is the relationship that he
has with him. A great many adoptive relations are translated into standard
kinship terms.

It was difficult to discover any traditional standards or values. From first
contact, there was a strong rejection of traditional ornaments and decorative objects; modern money and steel tools were quickly taken up. Other
evidence of opportunism and interest in the present were the Chimbus'
rapid adoption of new plants, their selling of trees and vegetables. They
were interested in every scheme for development, including some complete innovations, such as brick-making and wool-weaving. Whenever a
new business was proposed, the Chimbus had high expectations for it.
They planted passion fruit and other potential cash crops, were avid
gamblers and eagerly worked as domestic servants, police and laborers.
Chimbus would pick up shreds and fragments of the white man: tin-can
tops, pieces of metal and beads, rags, vests and paint were worn with pride.

There was always a search for variety, excitement and entertainment.
The normal economy and maintenance of domestic affairs occupies women
for many hours each day, but does not demand continuously heavy and
extensive male labor. The men were active in spurts and occasional bouts
of hard work: land preparation and garden fencing, house building or
ceremonial preparations. They could also devote their energies to prestige
building and to gaining in exchange and competition. Fighting — as a
raiding party attacking a lonely traveller — or joining battle against an
enemy group, was a source of pleasure and entertainment as well as loot.

Still another indication of this preoccupation with the present is their desire to have young people reach all the occupations and jobs now available — labor, domestic, technical, administrative and clerical. They were immediately attracted by new activities and goods of the white man. There was no restraint or feeling of incapacity or rejection.

These activities of stability or change are sometimes structured in movements. Thus, the reaction to contact may be resistance, isolation, or revival — a return to the past, as in the Plains Indian Ghost Dance. In Melanesia, the more common reaction was a great desire or 'hopeless envy' (Mair 1948) of the white man's goods, expressed in a cargo cult. But no fully-developed cargo cult has appeared in the highlands.

When the missionaries arrived, Chimbus flocked to the mission station. They enjoy the crowds and the activity of ritual and pageant. Some attend schools and services quite regularly and work energetically on mission projects, but I did not think them devout Christians. Little was said about Christianity and its principles, nor did I have any indication of expectation of rewards, on earth or in heaven, for Christian worship. As far as I could see, the church was not regarded with deep awe or reverence.

The Chimbus do not seem to idealize any period or form of culture — they seem to me to concentrate upon the life of the present, rarely thinking of the past, or seriously preparing for the future. Planning and execution never corresponded. No time or work schedules were attempted except under influence from European officers or employers.

They were delighted to accept the goods and new ways of the white man, discarding, replacing, embellishing or adding to their old things and practices. They did not readily compartmentalize their activities as 'before' and 'now,' or 'old Chimbu' and 'white man's'; rather, they lived in the present, recognizing that the only constant is change.

Chapter 3

The Kinds of Variation and Change

CHIMBU LIFE was always changing, but I think it would be possible to describe the pattern of culture as it existed in the period after sweet potatoes became the dietary staple, and before the Taylor-Leahy-Spinks Expedition opened the area up to western contact. Chimbu social life and group activity at this time can be characterized as mobile, with frequent fights, migrations and realignments. I shall attempt to describe the pattern within which modifications occurred, but it must be understood that some facets of Chimbu culture may have been more stable than others, and that these differences in stability cannot be identified without question.

This chapter presents a theory of social and cultural structure and change. While it is derived from the Chimbu case study, it is not without some potential wider application. Indeed, it appears to me that most anthropological generalizations are first proposed as based upon good first-hand knowledge of one or two societies and a slight or second-hand knowledge of others. The Chimbu case is poor in pre-history, but good in its short history. As a case study, it has both disadvantages and advantages for generalization about change. The Chimbu environment was not unchanging, but neither was it rapidly changing. There must have been variations in population growth, epidemics, droughts, and other environmental conditions. Cultural adaptation involved clearing the heavy forest trees for initial cultivation and the reversion, at first, of this former garden land into fallow. With an increase of population, agriculture became more intensive, with full clearing, drainage ditches, tillage, soil turnover and other land preparation techniques, the periods of cultivation

were more frequent, and a larger proportion of the land was under cultivation at any time. Planting casuarina trees during fallow, to restore soil
nutrients and provide useful timber must be taken as a significant advance
in the intensive use of the land. The use of stakes and fences along steep
hillsides to retain soil and stop land slippage was another important
development. The entire Chimbu agricultural complex permitted a high
population density on steep land (Brookfield and Brown 1963).

The Chimbu had a good sound knowledge of their environment, its
altitude, soil and crop variations, and their agriculture was adapted to this
intensive use of the environment. Local variations can be correlated with
the terrain, the soil type, and the crops planted.

The prehistoric evidence in the New Guinea highlands indicates a long
period of environmental adaptation with the same basic tool-kit: flaked
and ground stone blades and axes, wooden implements, weapons and some
bone artifacts. Many of the Chimbu manufactured goods are perishable.
These include bark cloth, woven fibre, fibre netting, and other clothing and
ornaments. The excavation of more recent sites may reveal more evidence
of bone, shell and wood artifacts. Stone quarries were not available every-
where; thus, there was some local variation, adapted, again, to the resources
available and to the needs of the local people.

Chimbu live at altitudes between 5,000 feet and 8,500 feet. Even so close
to the equator, it is cold, although rarely freezing, and the house walls and
roofs are thicker in the upper Chimbu valley than on the lower slopes.
Inside a Chimbu house a fire always smoulders, and it is built up for cooking and at night for warmth.

Local resources provide materials for houses, and the wood, matting and
grass used in the houses could be padded with additional thickness of
leaves and other material for insulation, and further, grass thatch could be
thickened or replaced from time to time.

There are many variations between individuals, decisions about actions,
such as the land chosen for cultivation, the crops which are planted on
this land, in the place of residence, and the actual location of a house,
the form of the house, participation in various group activities. We may
consider these to be individual choices among available, recognized cultural
alternatives. Not enough comparative study has been done to show the
extent of local or individual variation, in most matters, but our study of
settlement and residence (Brown and Brookfield 1967) indicates the many
types of variation in the Mintima area.

Community life may be a composite of actions and choice — it is an
interwoven complex, in which trends, choices, variations, and so on make
a constantly changing whole. A synchronic picture at any time is different

from that at any other time. Some elements of change may reverse, but the whole is never the same. For example, a statistical summary of the age of marriage, of the amount of land under crops, of the size of households, and of participation in a tribal ceremony, may show variation from time to time. But the conclusion that there are changing trends may not be warranted or provable.

It is particularly difficult to discern cycles from trends; cycles can only be isolated when a broad comparative series is available. But we must not expect the same kinds of cycles to be found in all societies. For example, in Chimbu, although there is some slight annual cycle in rainfall and a scarcely discernible cycle in temperature, this has no pronounced effect upon the agricultural cycle. Sweet potatoes are planted at nearly any time of the year, and harvested continuously once those in any particular plot begin to ripen. The only variations are a slight increase in intensity of land-clearing shortly before the onset of the rainy season, and an increase in land preparation and planting after a heavy rain, when the soil is more easily worked. Some gardens are cleared and planted and prepared at all times of the year. Chimbu have no seasonal harvest, and no harvest festivals. When preparing for a major feast, the specific time of year may not be of moment, but the group will endeavor to plant as rapidly as possible a sufficient crop of vegetable food so as to provide for the additional needs of the people, guests and animals during the period just before the major slaughter of pigs. This planting effort, then, is on an entirely different scale than provision for the annual food requirements of the family. Furthermore, food requirements of the family differ somewhat, depending upon the stage in the festival cycle which has been reached, since both people and pigs eat sweet potatoes. As the pig herd increases in numbers, and the pigs in the herd increase in size, more sweet potatoes are required. Again, a growing family will require larger gardens and bigger food crops. Furthermore, as some of the members of the family reach an age for special ceremonies or marriage, the need for added food crops may be anticipated by increased planting.

These types of change or variation are really of a different character than the sorts of change which occur when a society as isolated as Chimbu comes into contact with an entirely different tradition, such as that of the west. The immediate, startling impact of visitors from Australia was to present to the Chimbu a totally new complex of objects and a totally new group to which to adapt. Some traditional objects such as stone tools were almost immediately replaced by metal, and when other things such as blankets were seen, they were sought after and acquired as soon as possible. The desire was for useful and decorative items such as metal tools and household goods, towels, clothing, belts, new crops, imported salt, different shell ornaments, foods, and other additions and alternatives to traditional forms were readily accepted.

The Chimbu also frequently borrowed non-material items, such as customary practices, ceremonial activities, etc.

Perhaps the discussion can be clarified if we distinguish four kinds of variation and social change. There may of course be others, or some recombination of these may prove more helpful in understanding social processes, but my explication of Chimbu is suited to this division into four:

1. The interactional dynamic of social life — that is, the way that all human behavior, activities and relationships vary through choice, chance, situation, individuality — the sort of thing that Raymond Firth calls "social organization": variations and flux within what seems to be a pattern or structure of institutionalized social life. Such day-to-day variations and adaptations may, over a longer time, be one-directional trends, qualitatively or statistically assessable, but at any time of observation this is hardly discernible — perhaps an informant or anthropologist may predict that it is a trend, but its intensity is hard to judge.

Local, regional, or special circumstances, adaptations to differences in the natural or cultural environment, produce cultural alternatives or variations. We might call this internal variability, and comparative study may show that this is greater among some peoples than others; one would naturally expect it to be greater where there are more ethnic or cultural differences among peoples in contact — in trade relationships, border regions, multiethnic communities, etc. Dependence upon imported goods can only develop where trade is well established; local self-sufficiency or regional homogeniety are found where markets are absent.

2. Cycles or periodic changes exist within a larger uniformity: for example, the cycle of domestic family life, or land rotation and use, and of preparation for large-scale ceremonies. Many of these are biologically based: seasonal cycles and life cycles, of the earth, vegetation, crops and animals. Long-term cycles of land use and festivals, which may be a generation or longer in duration, can rarely be studied and assessed by the observing anthropologist. Such cycles or systems of cycles may be very complex; we found that within one Chimbu tribe, land use and the rotation of fallow and cultivation varied from one type of soil to another, and to some extent between subclans (Brookfield and Brown 1963).

3. Long-term trends include the evolutionary or developmental, one-directional, change from simple to complex forms. These may spring from basic inventions which stimulate many other developments, and significant introductions which are the beginnings of spurts of rapid change. Evolutionary growth may also be the cumulative sum of small changes and

trends, over a period of hundreds or thousands of years. Such developments result in a change from one form of society to another — food collecting to food producing, segmentary tribal structure to centralized state, feud to law, folk to urban, general to specialized occupational structure. Certainly such development is affected by contacts with other groups or their members, but over the long-term, internal development and the incorporation of these outside influences together produce a new basic pattern. The rate of change of aspects of society, or of society as a whole, may greatly vary. For example, in Tasmania and Australia, prehistoric remains of art, burials and some tools which have been dated 15,000-20,000 years ago are very similar to recent forms. Some New Guinea tool forms have been little changed, while others have dropped from use. Archaeological periods vary from a few years to thousands. There are examples from many parts of the world of a rapid change series and the accelerated introduction of wholly new forms. One change — technological, social or religious — may stimulate others to rapid development. We are not yet able to predict the force of such an innovation, or the extent to which it affects other aspects of culture.

4. The impact of an advanced technology and society upon a simple and isolated society. This is most dramatic, and most important today in the influence and domination of the west upon the hitherto isolated peoples outside Europe. In Chimbu the coming of the white man and colonial relationships has had a tremendous force, and the suppression of traditional cultural practices, introduction of education, new technology, new ideas, new forms of social organization, new diseases and crops, new forms of labor and relationships, new religious practices have all, within a few years, produced qualitative differences and trends of change. A large part of Chimbu technology and use of local materials has been replaced with imported items of clothing, ornaments, implements, and household materials. Tribal ceremonies have been greatly modified, and groupings now reflect the government-instituted census units, councillors' electorates, road work units, mission church groups, school districts, etc. The most influential of them have occurred during the intense contact of the past 35 years, but some effects of western contact through New Guinea intermediaries are hundreds of years old.

Chapter 4

Chimbu Pre-History[1]

THE PRE-HISTORY of New Guinea was virtually unknown fifteen years ago but in the past few years excavation and research dated with radiocarbon techniques suggest some tentative findings. Observations on New Guinea highlanders' physical characteristics and studies of their blood groups indicate that the people have a common origin and have been in their area for a long time.

There are some evidences that Chimbu and related people have been relatively isolated in the interior of New Guinea for thousands of years. Wurm's classification of languages (1961) distinguishes an East New Guinea Highlands Phylum and within this the East New Guinea Highlands Stock spoken by over 750,000 people. Chimbu is one of the largest language groups and is centrally located in the stock. They were probably not in direct contact with peoples of any other language stock. Even on trading expeditions, people commonly travel no farther than a neighboring tribe where they have friends; the object of trade may pass through many hands, but a person does not travel far from his tribe. The permanent remnant of such trade is most clearly seen in the shells and other durable objects. Some shells were traded into the New Guinea highlands nine thousand years ago. Trade must also be the source and route of plant varieties, styles of ornament, weapons and tool techniques, as well as beliefs and practices in social and ritual contexts. Contact among people speaking

[1] Peter White kindly read and commented upon this chapter in draft form. All the inaccuracies and misinterpretations that remain are mine.

different languages and of different cultural groups is limited to occasional visiting and trading in Melanesia, for Melanesians do not often venture where they have no kinsmen or trade associates. Persons outside their group are suspected of hostility, sorcery and vile practices, such as cannibalism. A stranger is never safe: his death and theft of his property are unlikely to be avenged. An adventurous man may develop contacts, friendships and marriage ties with people at some little distance who have some different ideas, goods or resources. Father A. Schaefer met such a man in Kavagl, who was visiting at Bundi, outside Chimbu, trading to obtain steel goods (Schaefer 1938). Such visits are sources of goods and practices which are the ebb and flow of cultural change.

The origins of man and his cultural advances — tool making and food production — are in the Old World. But the view that the center of development was the Near East has been questioned — much recent evidence shows important developments in Southeast Asia.

The first men crossed from Asia into Australia and New Guinea more than 30,000 years ago. The earliest sites in the New Guinea highlands yet known are rock shelters with materials 11,500 years old not far from the present Chimbu area. In the highlands the valley floors are over 4,000 feet in altitude, and both valley and slope over 6,000 feet were occupied. Some 10,000 years ago, the New Guinea highlands people lived by gathering wild vegetables, nuts and fruits and hunting. The largest animals were cassowary, a flightless bird, and marsupials. Most food was probably collected plants and small insects, birds, reptiles, marsupials and rats.

The flaked stone tools which are associated with the animal remains were probably mostly used for making wooden tools; but these wooden tools rarely survive. These artifacts were of extensive duration: flaked scrapers, often retouched, are common through thousands of years, from 11,500 years ago to the present.

Contemporary with these from perhaps 8000 B.C. are some new types of ground stone axe-adzes and 'waisted' flaked blades. In the New Guinea highlands these are striking examples of the continuity over a long time of two different traditions among the same people. The axe-adzes could be used for forest clearing, house and fence building, and the blade as a hoe or used to make a wooden hoe. From the analysis of pollen it seems that forest was cleared 5,000-6,000 years ago in the upper Wahgi valley (Powell 1970). This would suggest agriculture at this period. Direct evidence of agriculture — a wooden spade — has so far been found dating to 350 B.C. in the Wahgi area. Pigs are present in strata before 3000 B.C. Since the pigs must have been introduced as domesticated animals, this finding also supports the existence of a settled and food-producing economy at this time.

The entire Wahgi valley area, which is not now heavily populated, is covered with marks of former drainage ditches for a careful and advanced form of agriculture. The ditch system permits intensive cultivation in modern times, but population density 2,000 years ago remains in question. It is notable that the use of spades for tilling and digging rectangular ditches for draining is so ancient. Nowadays some parts of the western Wahgi are swampy, but this may not always have been the case. The basic crops 3,000 years ago, most likely, were taro, supplemented by yams, sugar cane, bananas, greens, beans and other vegetables and fruits (Brookfield 1971: 80 ff).

By the time they were discovered, the highlanders had taken over sweet potatoes as their main crop. Sweet potato is of South American origin and both historical and botanical evidence lead to the conclusion that it was introduced to the Philippines and then to New Guinea after the 16th century. Such a replacement of the basic crop does not seem to be improbable. In South America, banana and plantain became staple foods for Orinoco tribes (Chagnon 1968); maize and manioc have become staples in Africa. The sweet potato produces a good food staple for man and his pigs in tropical highlands, and permits a high population density at higher altitudes than any native New Guinea food crop. New Guinea highlanders are enthusiastic gardeners, always interested in new plants. They quickly began to cultivate corn, pumpkin, beans, peanuts and other crops. Many of these have been introduced since the white man first came to New Guinea, and some of them reached the highlands through trade between natives before the white man reached the highlands.

Later than the beginning of agriculture, but before sweet potatoes, are other ground stone objects: club heads, figurines, mortars and pestles. These have been found widely in New Guinea, but except for the club heads, still made in mountain regions both to the east (Blackwood 1950) and at Mt. Bosavi in Papua, the time range of their manufacture is uncertain. Many have been found and considered curios or of magical value by modern New Guineans who knew nothing of their former use.

The archaeological record is still limited to a few sites and varies so from site to site that it cannot yet be fully interpreted. Chimbu were far from the world centers of technological and political development. Before 1933, they were the end point of many trade routes leading inland from the coast. They valued shells, feathers and plumes, especially from the bird of paradise, which was found in the forest and some open areas, but rarely in the main areas in which they lived. Although they had dwelt in the highland valleys for many thousands of years, a large part of their cultural equipment had reached them from sources outside New Guinea and many valued goods were obtained from other New Guinea peoples.

I cannot resist adding my own composite statement on New Guinea highlands culture history, especially as it relates to understanding of the Chimbu. The convergence of my interpretation and those of other anthropologists will be evident.

The earliest people in the New Guinea highlands, 10,000 or more years ago, were gatherers, collectors and hunters using bone, flaked and perhaps ground stone tools, eating wild plant foods, and obtaining animals by hunting, snares and traps. They used rock shelters and caves occasionally for cooking, resting or sleeping. It is in these caves and rock shelters that archaeologists may find the evidences of this early period.

Perhaps 5,000-6,000 years ago, gardening began and pigs were introduced from lowland regions where they had spread. Some variety of crops was grown but very likely taro became the most important (Barrau 1965), and cultivated foods replaced wild foods as the mainstay of the diet. These highland gardens were probably limited to areas beneath 6,500 feet in altitude and concentrated on the larger valley floors where some tillage, ditching or other preparation of the soil was practiced. Pigs, which probably entered New Guinea as domestic animals, were kept, gardens were fenced to protect them from pigs, and perhaps pigs were only partly fed by the people. Many of the tools were similar to those used in preagricultural times. The ground stone axe was used in forest clearing and the blade, attached to a handle, for soil preparation. Mortars, pestles, figurines and club heads of volcanic stone were known and used in some ways. These may have been traded into the highlands, although some were manufactured there. The mortars and pestles were probably used for grinding seeds, nuts or other materials which may have been used as food, medicine, poison or pigment. Valley floors were drained and tilled for easier food production. No regular alternation of cultivation and fallow was established; the gardens were replanted as required.

I assume that this agricultural adaptation stimulated population increase and a gradual intensification of agriculture. This involved a short or nonexistent fallow period, but it is questionable whether more or less or the same amount of labor was involved in the preparing of land and growing the crop as agriculture became more intensive (Boserup 1965). By 2,500 years ago in the lower valleys, particularly the Wahgi and the Goroka areas, there were developed intensive cultivation techniques, fencing, terracing, mounding, ditching, tillage, planting trees and fallow crops for nutrient and moisture control. There was probably an increase in population and interaction of population and food supply increase leading to greater intensification, more developed agriculture techniques and denser populations. Through fighting and population movements and migration, the population was redistributed and spread among and between the mountains and valleys of the area. Groups were in competition for resources.

I do not pretend here to assess the relationship between the cultures of the highlands of East New Guinea and of West Irian, where some similar developments apparently have taken place. Nor do I attempt to guess when highlands people spilled over the Wahgi-Sepik Divide to inhabit the Jimi and other valleys on the northern side of the mountains. A complex of physical, archaeological, and linguistic data is required for this. Comparing highlands peoples, we can distinguish a variety of agricultural techniques and techniques of pig domestication, settlement, distribution of houses, gardens, fences and grazing lands, resources, altitude, technology, disease patterns and many other things. The variation was not only cultural, it also involved variations in environmental factors. Malaria become a problem in the lower valleys, with effects upon population distribution and morbidity. Forests were partly depleted, and grassland established in the open valley areas of the Asaro and Wahgi. I believe the general scale of groups at this time to have been smaller than at the present.

The introduction of the sweet potato, perhaps 350 years ago, and its spread has had drastic and dramatic changes; but I do not consider that these are quite as revolutionary as Watson (1965) does. Sweet potatoes made possible population concentration at a much higher altitude (Bowers 1971). The slope cultivation, with terracing, fencing, tillage and ditches, produced a dense population above 6,000 feet in the Chimbu area. To the west, drainage ditches, tillage, mounding, mulching and composting were utilized. There may have been some changes in the distribution of settlement at this time. For example, in the Chimbu area, the men's houses were located at high lookout points for defense, whereas secure sites for the houses of women and children were provided by hiding them in lower areas. There was a balance in the dangers of attack or epidemics and the requirements for gardening and pig care. To the east, village or hamlet settlement in more open valleys was usual, with fewer trees, less intensive land preparation and lower population density. The amount of food and shelter provided for pigs varies, and thus we might say they are less domesticated in some fringe areas. There was a further intensification of agriculture in many places and a development of some specialized techniques, such as the open fields of sweet potatoes in the western highlands which were under more permanent forms of cultivation than other kinds of gardens. Intensification of agriculture involved the continued use of the same land for several crops with a shorter fallow period or an intermittent fallow period and the use of soil conservation techniques. In Chimbu and in some other areas, casuarina trees were grown during fallow and this further provided both wood and nutrient to the soil. This seems to have developed after sweet potatoes and slope cultivation were established.

Casuarina breeds naturally in moist places, such as stream beds. The seedling is carried and replanted in gardens by Chimbus.

There was an increasing scale of groups in development of tribal organization and intertribal exchanges and fights. The fighting weapons were the bow and arrow, spear and axe. Fighting was undertaken for vengeance, compensation, pig theft and in marriage relations in all areas of the highlands. Some fights led to migration, displacement, conquest, crop destruction, etc., but competition for land was not the sole cause of fighting or land acquisition the frequent result of the fighting. Furthermore, fighting seems to have been just as frequent and destructive amongst those people who were not densely settled as it was among those who were. Land scarcity and land competition were not the only factors involved in the highlands warfare. Nevertheless, territorial redistribution occurred. People were driven from their territory and avoided dwelling close to others because of their fears of retaliation, sorcery, poisoning, cursing, witchcraft, etc. (Reay 1959).

Some people reduced their fallow period to a permanent field planting: in sweet potato culture this involves taking the crop from the ground over a long period of time and repreparation and planting of the land in an irregular fallow which varies from months to years. This is not necessarily a general, intentional, or systematic pattern of shortening fallow and intensifying agriculture. Indeed, there are many short-term reasons and special requirements under which a fallow period might be shortened. For example, a widow who has little or no help to clear new large garden areas may continue to use a garden which she has already prepared, even though its yield may somewhat decline over time. When her sons grow up, they will clear new land for her, or if she marries again, her husband may do so. Meanwhile, she uses what she has. People abandon some areas in illness or in conflict and intensify their use of some areas because they do not want to go elsewhere. Ageing people cultivate areas already in use rather than work new clearings. At times of intense hostility between groups, gardens are concentrated in the center of their territory, away from the borders subject to attack.

This interpretation of the general history of the New Guinea highlands raises many new questions about cultural variations in population distribution as they exist in the present and recent past. For in the highlands there is much diversity in climate, altitude, rainfall, soils, etc., which limits some crops and the density of settlement.

The upper Chimbu valley was cultivated to an altitude of 9,000 feet, yet in the adjacent Asaro valley the upper limit of cultivation was 8,000 feet (Brookfield 1964). Physical factors may not be the sole explanation. The use of an area for gardens or houses may be affected by what the people think about the productivity of land, the dangers of frost, enemies, spirits or disease. Thus any settlement is affected not only by a multiplicity of physical, ecological and technological factors but by social patterns and beliefs which can run counter to reality. For example, the Chimbu avoided the lower altitude grasslands of the Wahgi valley and believed that the land is poor in the moisture necessary to produce good sweet potatoes. According to Chimbu, it is inhabited by dangerous wild spirits that bring disease and death. Further, the bodies of people who died of certain dreaded diseases have been thrown into holes there, so a combination of their diseases and their spiritual influence is dangerous, especially to their relatives. When the mission acquired some of this land and grew successful crops there, Chimbus were surprised and wanted more compensation, because the land was better than they had thought. Beliefs change and the demonstration that no harm came made some Chimbus regret the loss, even though they would not have used the land earlier.

Similarly, malaria seems to have spread up the Wahgi valley in recent decades. It is still rare in the higher altitudes of the Chimbu and Koro valleys and in the Eastern Highlands District. But the open Wahgi valley was avoided as a source of disease. It is this area, now swampy, in the western Wahgi valley which from marks of ancient ditches and archaeological evidence was much more heavily populated in the past. This earlier dense population, it seems, must have predated the sweet potato. If taro was the main staple, it requires more moisture and warmth than sweet potato, and is more suited to the moister valley floor.

The grasslands of the Eastern Highlands District may have been created by burning for cultivation as Robbins (1963) believes. It is possible that they have been cultivated longer than the Wahgi valley or that they have been burned more in war, or that the climate or other conditions prevent the regeneration of bush and forest (Brookfield 1964). The casuarina planting of Chimbu was for conservation and for wood. The Asaro people on the whole use less wood in their houses and fences than do the Chimbu. These flimsier fences must not be subject to the same ravages of hungry pigs as are Chimbu fences. A lower human population density and larger pig forage area would satisfy this need.

The special characteristics of sweet potato, which has been the basis of subsistence in the highlands, may have had a great effect in the distribution of people within the highlands. The Telefolmin area, where taro is the staple, has no such high altitude gardens, and a sparse population. Although the population may have been more dense in some areas where the main food was taro and mixed vegetables, the population must have been concentrated below 6,000 feet. High altitude gardens on steep slopes must be mainly sweet potatoes, with some subsidiary crops. In particular, the upper Chimbu valley and the Koro valley of the Chimbu District, and the Wabag area could probably not support their present densities on the pre-sweet potato crops or without special techniques of drainage, mulching and soil renewal. But the Huli of Tari at 5,300 feet on open country, with a lower density today, may have been as dense or nearly so with the taro subsistence base (Glasse 1968).

There is much difference, too, between people and their recognition of land adequacy and scarcity. The Huli, objectively and subjectively, have plenty of land, the Central Enga very little. We have developed a formula for calculating occupation density on the basis of the possible carrying capacity of land with a given economy and technology. Occupation at full capacity is 1.0. (Brookfield & Brown 1963). In Chimbu, the tribal traditions indicate a migration from the dense valley to the more open and even now only moderately occupied areas south and west. I believe this movement to have been wthin the last 200 to 300 years, that is, since the sweet potato became the staple food.

Still later some other crops have been added to the highlands collection. Tobacco, corn and some other varieties of vegetables reached the highlands before the first exploratory expedition. And since the white man has been there, beans, peas, potatoes, pumpkins, cabbage and peanuts and many other minor fruits and vegetables have been added to provide variety and improve nutrition. The introduction of cash crops has of course had a great effect on land, life and economic relations.

In Chimbu, there have been over 2,000 years of agriculture and increasing population density, yet this seems not to have centralized political control or accumulated wealth. There were always big and small tribes, big men and transactional activities at all levels. Chimbu has had many centuries of land shortage; fights and expansion, migration and resettlement.

There was no surplus or accumulation of wealth or use of economic advantage to change the political or economic system. There were always big men, competitions, rivalry, but no permanent advantages — no conquest, centralization, or political dominance. Furthermore, if we compare Chimbu to the less densely settled groups in the highlands, we do not see any substantial centralization as a result of the very much greater density in Chimbu than among their neighbors.

There is a characteristic scale and size of group organizing for a range of different types of activities in Chimbu, from the informal gathering and food sharing of a men's house to large periodic pig feasts of tribes. All of these festive occasions require products of the land: vegetable food and pigs. The requirements of a family for food and its land may change as the family grows or becomes depleted, and they are also responsive to the clan and tribe plans for major feasts, as well as for the individual obligations of members of the household towards their kinsmen to supply them with food or pigs or valuables for their important occasions. Individual and family demands on the land and on produce fluctuate and each family has its own growth cycle: grandparents die as grandchildren grow up. A tribe's dependence upon its land's productivity may vary with the large cycle of periodic pig feasts, since the pig feast requires raising large numbers of pigs and providing them with considerably increased quantities of food during the time which they are being prepared for a feast. Normal family — human and pig — food needs are affected by its participation in the periodic large feasts. Such pressures, fluctuating as they do over long periods of time, may well have effects upon the systems of land tenure and agricultural practices. They may force a more intensive form of agriculture, and new techniques of cultivation. In this way, the everyday satisfying of personal needs, for food and other products and the cycles of agriculture and animal husbandry lead to social and cultural change.

Chapter 5

Chimbu's First Contact with Europeans

CHIMBU HAVE LIVED for thousands of years in the highlands of New Guinea. Densely settled on steep hillsides and narrow valleys, they had been discovering, adapting, inventing, modifying, trading with and learning from neighboring peoples to develop to the Chimbu society of 1933. There were contacts with outsiders on the coast which had repercussions in social reaction and culture change in Chimbu before 1933. In the last years some few objects of western manufacture reached them through trade with neighboring mountain peoples. We cannot be sure of any direct contact with outsiders (see Willis 1969) until Leahy, who in his first (1931) exploration of the Eastern highlands discovered the Dunantina, Asaro and Bena valleys. Then the Taylor, Leahy and Spinks expedition was organized in 1933. Working westward through hitherto unknown regions, they reached the Chimbu area, north of the Wahgi, early in April and from that time onwards we can follow some kind of occasionally written record of the Chimbu.

The reports of administrative officers and missionaries are valuable from many points of view as a record of events and a description of conditions. They reflect the concerns and attitudes of the writers and the impression made by Chimbu upon their literate visitors. Thus Leahy says:

Before we left Wau, I had the good fortune to meet three of Taylor's superiors in the administration, and seized the opportunity to promote as strongly as possible his project for an official patrol into the newly-discovered valley. It was eventually arranged that the expedition should be a joint one, Taylor and his detail of police representing Authority and Danny [Leahy's younger brother] and I and our boys, with the surveyor, Spinks, representing Commercial Enterprise. Our overland party was to be backed up by planes, which would be available for reconnaissance flights and would fly out supplies and trade goods to landing fields which we would build. It was as good a plan of exploration as could have been worked out for the task in view.

On March 8, 1933, with the veteran pilot I. Grabowsky at the controls, Major Harrison and I and my brothers, Jim and Dan, flew out over the new valley and laid to rest for all time the theory that the center of New Guinea is a mass of uninhabitable mountains. What we saw was a great, flat valley, possibly twenty miles wide and no telling how many miles long, between two high mountain ranges, with a very crooked river meandering through it. Below us were evidence of a fertile soil and a teeming population — a continuous patchwork of gardens, laid off in neat squares like checkerboards, with oblong grass houses, in groups of four or five, dotted thickly over the landscape. Except for the grass houses, the view below us resembled the patchwork fields of Belgium, as seen from the air. Certainly the 50,000 or 60,000 new people we had found on the upper Purari were as nothing compared to the population that must live in this valley. When consideration of our gasoline supply forced us to turn back, the westward limits of the valley were still lost in the haze of distance.

The results of that flight made front-page news all over the world, and hastened preparations for an overland expedition. Supplies were flown out to our landing field on the Bina Bina, and presently Taylor marched into camp at the head of his police, as thoroughly pleased with the outlook as a small boy going to a picnic. Before setting out, we made one more reconnaissance flight out over the valley, with Tom O'Day as pilot and the white personnel of the expedition as passengers. This time we flew right up the valley to within sight of a great table-topped mountain that seemed to mark the western end of it, though visibility was not too good and the valley broadened out so far to the north and south that we could not be certain of its limits. The flat and thickly populated area appeared to be roughly sixty miles long by twenty miles broad — an island of population so effectively hemmed in by mountains that the rest of the world had not even suspected its existence.[1]

I shall trace what happened in Chimbu since the Taylor, Leahy and Spinks expedition which crossed through this Wahgi valley area in 1933, supported and supplied by New Guinean and Papuan police and carriers. As far as we know, the word "Chimbu" was used as a greeting and also was applied to the Chimbu River (Leahy 1937). But since that time, the 60,000 people of the Chimbu and Koro river valleys and the intervening region have been known as "Chimbu" to themselves and others, both Europeans and natives of other regions. In other parts of the Papua New Guinea, "Chimbu" means all people of the District, and often all high-landers.

[1] Leahy and Crain 1937: 150-1.

We shall never know precisely what the Chimbus thought at the first sight of the expedition, but we know that Leahy concluded from the action of one of the women that she believed that one of the native members of the exploratory group was the reincarnation of a lost relative. The unprecedented appearance of an expedition of white and black strangers made a tremendous impression upon the people. The Chimbu have certainly never been the same since.

A small group of the exploratory expedition, left near the Koro river to keep a post and makeshift landing field, was much harassed by natives attempting to steal their goods. Later the expedition was attacked for their possessions — the shells, steel tools and other objects. Chimbus were soon to learn of rifle power, for on the return trip when Taylor was attacked by natives he used guns to defend himself. This first visit by outsiders was rapidly followed by many more visits and by the settlement in the area of several kinds of strangers. Among the first were missionaries, both Catholic and Lutheran. Several mission stations were established in 1934 — Catholics at Mirani (near Kundiawa), at Kurugu, close to the present Mingende mission, and at Goglme in the Chimbu valley; Lutherans at Ega, adjacent to Kundiawa on the lower Chimbu river and at Kerowagi in the Koro valley. Of course, missionaries had some small store of manufactured goods which they used for gifts and for trade, but very quickly the Chimbu took a great interest in obtaining these goods, these properties of the white man. In December, 1934, and in January, 1935, only months after the first Catholic missions were established, two similar and serious incidents occurred. The Chimbu had stolen goods from the storage rooms of the missions and burnt mission houses. When the thefts were discovered, the mission officials responded by taking property and shooting pigs belonging to the Chimbus. Then, in retaliatory attacks, two missionaries in two separate locations were injured and both later died.

As soon as the news was known, Australian officials were sent to investigate. This initiated the administrative suppression of killing, and quickly established colonial domination and superiority of the white man over the natives. The killings did not go unpunished; Chimbus were taken into prison and made to see that the white man would not tolerate theft or wounding or killing. Tribal fights were stopped and participants arrested. After this, Australian administrative posts always preceded the missions in newly discovered areas. The Chimbu learned to fear the white man's weapons.

From 1935 there were several Chimbu posts, both Lutheran and Catholic mission establishments, and police and government officers under the Australian administration. Throughout the remainder of the 1930's there were further incidents involving the white men, theft of their manufactured goods by natives, attack and retaliations. Chimbus are immensely curious about the white man and his goods. Taylor noted that they were at first friendly to Europeans and later more self-confident, truculent, demanding or stealing goods, especially the shells used for trade and much valued by the Chimbus.

The chief aim of the Australian administration was to establish communications and a peaceful order. A major concern was to stop the tribal fighting which had been normal and frequent throughout the area. Fighting arose from disputes and thefts — the first step of the "Pax Australiana" was to replace fighting with the officer's court of justice. Wrongdoers were sent to jail. Soon the Chimbus appeared to show confidence in the white man and to trust in their relations with him. Manufactured goods, especially axes, knives and shovels, became common.

Road work — the clearing of tracks as a "highway" — was an important requirement to insure that the Australian officers and local people could quickly traverse the main routes throughout the region interconnecting the government and mission posts. Missionaries and government officers began to ride horses and to urge the introduction of breeding horses. Clearings were made for airfields and supplies brought in by plane. For many years the big inland posts were not connected to the coastal administrative centers by motor road.

The reports of the 1930's are of some interest in understanding the view that the white man had of the Chimbus and to give us some record of the activities, the problems, the building of roads and bridges, the troubles between mission and Chimbu and between different groups of Chimbu. However, these reports were never full. Indeed, among the remarks by the Australian officer (*kiap*) were that the office (*hauspepa*) was short of paper so that reports had to be curtailed. Very little work in depth could be done with the local people. All communication was through uneducated Pidgin English-speaking interpreters. Some censuses were taken in the 1930's and 1940's, but at first only a fraction of the population actually came in to be counted. The latest (1970) population figure for Chimbu District is 185,295. The population is now growing rapidly.

Some use was made of native leaders in establishing contact and relationships between the local groups and the administration. The native leaders were asked to report disputes and fights to the administration so that war and fights could be prevented or stopped. The first recognized leaders were unofficial *bosbois*. Later some of these leaders were appointed as *luluai* following the system of native officials used throughout New Guinea. Many of these were fight leaders who spent a term "retraining" in jail.

Papuan and New Guinean policemen and interpreters were the usual intermediaries; had we records of their experience and relations with the highlands people, they would surely be of great interest and value. Our chief sources are reports written by the Australian government officer in the main station at Kundiawa. Some accounts were written by missionaries with anthropological training (Nilles, Schaefer, Aufenanger). Our information is scantier on the teachers and medical officers who were at the Chimbu post during the 1930's and 1940's. For a year or two, there was a government school at Kundiawa, but this was closed during World War II. Catholic and Lutheran mission schools provided some basic as well as religious instruction, and medical service was given both by mission and government. Indeed, the Chimbus did not clearly distinguish mission from government in the early years — both represented the source of new things, practices and regulations.

However, many of these activities were curtailed during the Second World War when the Australian administration established a military government, ANGAU. Australian officers were posted in the stations, and maintained administration under military command. No fighting or Japanese troops reached the highlands and the only visible remainder of the war were a few fragments of a fallen plane which had become decorative trophies at a number of houses.

In the post-war period, administrative, medical and educational services have slowly increased. Since 1946 there have been more complete census and other records and information about the local people. After the war, the New Guinea territory was transferred to a United Nations Trusteeship and from that time onward the United Nations has sent investigating missions to make reports on the progress of the entire territory.

Perhaps the next major influence was the Highlands Labor Scheme, which developed a program for taking young men to work for a term of two years outside the district. Fifty or sixty percent of the men in some groups were recruited for this work, but the normal average was 15-20%. Men were taken by road and by air out of the highlands area, and given work mainly on coastal plantations as laborers. They were fed and housed, but received most of their wages at the end of the contract, when they bought goods and carried their purchases and some money home. Their work gave them new experience and contact with strangers; they visited towns and saw "salt water" for the first time. By 1960, most young adult Chimbu men had spent some time away at work in highlands areas if not on the coast.

The agricultural extension program in 1955 and afterwards promoted coffee as a cash crop. This has become Chimbu's largest commercial activity, with a buying cooperative. Fruit and vegetable growing of newly introduced as well as established crops for local sale has developed, too. Money has been used increasingly for native exchange, taxes and purchase of goods for investment and consumption. There was a rapid development of coffee production from 1958 to 1965, but prices and sales fluctuated during this period. Technological change, marketing and the consumption of European manufactured goods did not develop at the same rate as coffee production.

In 1959, a local government council was established and elected local councillors. At first four Chimbu tribes and later a larger combined council met to discuss current political, economic and social issues and recommend legislation. During the 1960's a representative House of Assembly was established and Chimbus have participated in national elections. Independence is now planned, but without a constitution or definite date.

The significant developments which have occurred in technology, education, health, law, government, religion and the economy will be discussed in later chapters.

Chapter 6

Domestic and Local Groups

THIS DISCUSSION of the dynamics of tribal life begins by examining the interplay between an individual's personal relationships and transactional activities and his participation in tribe, clan or segment activities. Further discussion of group composition follows.

The people of the Chimbu valley, at the beginning of the 20th century, were densely settled on their steep hills. Men clustered together in large houses on high lookout sites, the men and boys of the local group sharing the house and serving as a defensive force against enemies. Each married woman, her unmarried daughters, young sons and also the family's pigs,[1] were resident in one or more houses some distance from the larger men's house.

Women's houses were usually located in the family gardens or on the fringe of a garden area with a fenced pathway into the land in which the pigs foraged. Fences throughout the Chimbu area separate the land currently in use for gardens from the land in which pigs are allowed to range freely for forage. Houses, gardens and forage are scattered throughout the territory. There is no need to herd pigs, for they are fenced out of garden areas and come back to houses for feeding at night. When the best sweet potatoes have been taken from a garden, pigs are brought into it and tethered. They eat the remaining sweet potatoes, other plants, roots and insects, and turn over the soil.

---

[1] The sharing of houses by women, children and pigs in Chimbu might be thought unusual, but it should be recalled that Hungarian men sleep in the stables (Fel and Hofer 1968).

Each family has rights to land in a number of sections of the subclan territory. The several garden areas are often on different soils and at different altitudes or slopes, and suitable for various crops. Thus, each family has a share in the subclan's range of land types. While sweet potatoes grow on nearly every kind of land in Chimbu, sugar cane and bananas and some vegetables have a more restricted range. The rare and highly-valued pandanus trees, of two types, oil and nut, require different types of land: the oil pandanus trees occur singly in garden and fallow land below 6,000 feet and the nut pandanus are grown in groves, or found wild, at altitudes over 6,000 feet.[2]

Chimbu men and women, husbands and wives, are rarely seen together as couples — they work and sleep apart. In domestic and social activities they take different roles and are usually accompanied by others of the same sex. Women sit with their youngest children in a group, preparing vegetable food for cooking, carrying goods in their netbags; men arrange and distribute the food and valuables, butcher and cook pork.

Sexual separateness is not expressed in such sharp opposition or belief in danger and hostility, however, as has been reported in some Melanesian societies. Both men and women avoid close and continuous contact with the opposite sex. The men believe this is dangerous to their well-being and fear the ridicule of other men if they spend too much time with their wives in the evening. They normally return to the men's house after the late afternoon meal which they share with wife and children at the women's house. Women, on their part, seem to enjoy both their close relations with other women and families in their neighborhood, and their separate home life with children. Often a childless woman has children stay with her or hosts a small courting party of one or two neighborhood girls and a few visiting young men. Sexual separateness seems to be declining: men's houses no longer are a necessary defense against enemy attacks, and mission teaching, or other forces changing beliefs may be lessening the fear of pollution from women.

As he grows up, a person is increasingly involved in a personal network of social relationships and transactional ties. A child is born in a tiny birth hut, which his father has built for his mother, usually on the father's land, and quite close to the mother's house of residence. He spends his first two or three years mainly with his mother, being carried to her garden and other activities in a net bag and almost constantly in her care. He is not weaned until he is three years or older; only then do his parents resume sexual intercourse. Thus births are spaced at four years or more (Brown and Winefield 1965). From the age of three or four, a boy accompanies his

[2] A full discussion of agriculture and group territories will be found in Brookfield and Brown 1963.

father some of the time, and of course plays with other small children in
the local area. His closest contacts are with the families of other men in
his father's men's house and subclan, for these men's wives and children
inhabit most of the houses nearby. Among these families there is some cooperative gardening, help in preparation of food, sharing of food for feasts
and celebrations, and occasional attendance at larger-scale festivities. From
about the age of six, he spends most of his nights at his father's men's
house, often playing during most of the day with the boys who are the sons
of other men in this house, and eventually growing up to form an age group
of teenaged boys, firstly from his own men's house and secondly from
other men's houses in his subclan and clan. In adolescence, he attends
courting parties with his age mates in his own clan and tribe. As a boy,
he often visits his matrilateral kin, his married sisters, his other kinsmen,
his affines, and the kinsmen and affines of other boys in his group, scattered
in the surrounding clans. Chimbus often visit, and sometimes spend many
years, with relatives outside of their clan group. In the uncertain life of
Chimbu, the death of a father, remarriage of a mother to another subclan,
flight of the family in warfare, and close attachment of a man to certain
of his kin and affines, all lead to many attachments of a young person to
his kin or older men in his clan outside his own immediate family.

The young males of a subclan, or set of subclans using the same ceremonial ground, were initiated as a group at a time just before a large pig
ceremony. Since these pig ceremonies are held about every seven to ten
years, the boys to be initiated fall into a considerable age range, and this can
hardly be a group of close age mates being initiated. Chimbu initiates are
made to feel much discomfort but little severe pain. Youths recognize age
mates in the subclan and clan as those who go on courting parties together
and are companions in other activities. The large courting parties to visit
girls in another tribe and attendance at pig feasts bring together the young
men of the several clans of a tribe. They prepare and practice songs in
advance for these occasions.

Most young men have close ties to their father or other older men in
their father's men's house and subclan group. In the absence of a living
father, most boys can count upon the assistance of some other older clansman as a foster father to help him marry and become established. But a
close mother's brother, or another kind of kinsman, or a sister's husband,
may serve the same kind of foster-parent function. The leading older men,
or 'big men,' very often are foster fathers or sponsors of a number of
young men whose fathers are dead or incapable of carrying out the obligations themselves. The younger man needs help in accumulating the shells,
feathers, axes, money and pigs for a marriage payment, and older persons
must find a young woman whose older relatives are satisfied with the pay-

ment offered, and will proceed to arrange the marriage. At the age of about 20 or 22, a young man is suddenly launched into adult life, with a wife, a great many obligations to those who provided his marriage payment, and a set of new affines as his most important exchange partners. Even if he marries a girl of his choice, the obligations are heavy and increase as children are born.

A youth begins to live and work with an older man, normally with his father if he is alive. Brothers jointly inherit their father's land, which includes trees and garden land in crops, and rights to fallow, forest and bush. But a man may be associated with others, both more distant agnates in the subclan section, and kin or affines in other clans, especially neighboring clans. Such ties arise as a free choice within a somewhat restricted range, and in this way each man develops his own close associates, in intense mutual aid, from whom he obtains garden plots and becomes identified with a men's house group. Close ties and dwelling in the same men's house are common between a young man and an older man — his father or foster father. Brothers often continue to share land claims and sometimes prepare gardens for their wives together on joint land, but such joint activity is also frequent among men in the subclan section who together clear and prepare, and then divide the land of one of them, or prepare adjacent plots which they each claim. Such cooperation does not result in a merging of households. The result is neither rigid subgroup exclusiveness nor idiosyncratic social networks, but a choice of associates from the subgroup and non-agnatic kinsmen and affines.

After marriage, a man becomes a full householder and gardener. He may have a few small plots of land before, but he begins to prepare larger gardens on land which he has inherited or acquired from his father and older men of his subclan, and perhaps from kinsmen outside. Most of these plots become his land, to be used again whenever he chooses to do so. A house is built for his wife and his pigs on this land, and in this gardening and housebuilding work, he is helped by other men, mostly of his men's house and subclan.

The continuity of life for a girl is, of course, strikingly different. After growing up with her mother, usually in her father's subclan area, she is taken from this household by her husband's group at marriage. The bride usually lives with an older woman of her husband's group for some months before a separate house is built for her and the couple begins to have sexual intercourse and forms an independent household with its gardens and pigs. In polygamous marriages each wife has her own house and gardens. We found a number of cases in which a joint compound household of father and son with their wives persisted for years after marriage, usually with separate houses for each married woman. These also are found when the older couple is partially incapacitated and dependent upon the younger; such an older couple may be attached to their married daughter and her husband, using the land of either man, and sometimes both. A widowed parent is similarly also often part of a household.

The young couple receives some help from these older associates of the husband, but it is the husband's own responsibility to keep his wife from running away, to encourage her to take proper care of the pigs, to produce food for the family and to plan for the exchanges and distributions upon which his future success depends. His closest associates are those men who live in his men's house, garden adjacent plots, cooperate with him in work, housebuilding, and providing for ceremonies which are planned by a larger group. Each man has his own set of associates, kinsmen, affines and exchange partners, but those who live and work together form a core which may join with other groups for the larger-scale activities. Each man then has his own personal set of obligations and relationships, and also obligations to support the other men in his men's house and subclan and tribe, for larger ceremonial activities and rivalry between the larger groups, such as clans and tribes. In 1958, among a group of 206 adult men, after one or more marriages, divorces and widowhoods, 9% had no wife, 81% had one wife, 9% had two wives and 1% had three wives. Mission influence has reduced the frequency of polygyny.

Households merge for short periods of visiting, and when a family migrates to join affines or kin, they reside with and share food with their hosts for some time until they establish gardens and build houses. Adjustments are made in households to care for aged and incapacitated persons who join kin. What appears to be polygyny is often an extension of a man's domestic realm to include a widow and her children as a separate sub-household: the man builds a house and prepares gardens for the widow and fosters her children. Less frequently, a widower with children becomes attached to another household. Some widows remain more independent and maintain a separate household with a minimum of assistance from the men of their husband's group, or return to their agnates for assistance.

During 1959 and 1960, garden work parties were very common, and I recorded the names and relationships of the helpers on twenty-seven occasions. But this kind of cooperative activity was less frequent during my other periods of field work. Leaders often initiate large-scale group activities, such as a large garden made by a number of men in order to provide a feast. Cooperative work groups vary from a few men to perhaps thirty, called by a garden owner to help him clear trees and growth, and make fences and ditches in preparation for his garden. When the fence separating gardens from pig-forage land is to be built, or major repairs are needed, all the men whose land is enclosed are expected to help. But work parties for one family's garden clearing and ditch digging are usually made up of a few men or women of the garden owner's subclan, plus some relatives such as brothers-in-law, daughters, sisters or cousins of the women, or their husbands, and neighbors who are of other subclans. When the garden is ready for planting, the wives of the helpers may be given a section for their own use. Large and small work parties carry out the job without leadership or direction: each person works on a section and moves to other areas until the whole garden is cleared, ditches dug, etc.

House building is an arduous activity, in which the framework timbers must be cut and placed by a group of men working together. For a wife's house, the husband usually has help from a few of his close associates. The further work of putting up the stakes and making matting for the walls, poles and thatch for the roof, may be done with help, or, more slowly, by the man alone. A woman's contribution to house building is usually limited to cutting grass for thatching and bringing it to the site. Women's houses are built in the area currently in use for gardens. They are usually on a new site.

A men's house is larger, and usually put up by a group of men who are attached to the group which centers on the hilltop or cliff site. Often, a house is on the same clearing, to replace an old and rotting house. We calculated (Brown and Brookfield 1967:130) the life of houses as averaging about four years. At one house replacement in 1959, which was organized by a prominent elder, on one day, eleven men and youths who planned to live in the new house worked. Three other men helped, but only planned to stay there now and then, and another four helped but did not intend to use the house. Others came and went, helping a bit. Late in the day, eight wives brought cooked sweet potatoes to serve the workers. Another day, only four men were working and several women brought thatch for the roof. Two months earlier, I watched another house building — only three men planned to live there, but they had eleven helpers, and five women besides their wives brought food. Over the months and years, there was a core of almost permanently resident men and a larger number of men who moved from one house to another or on a succession of visits according to their local activities, work patterns, ties to relations, state of health and other factors.

Chapter 7

Groups and Segments

CHIMBU ENVISAGE their group structure as one of patrilineal segments. The largest group is described as having had a founder, and subgroups at each level are regarded as the sons of the founder. The links between the levels in this hierarchy are also conceived as those between brothers and between fathers and sons. But ordinarily only one level or the relations between two levels are under consideration. Therefore, a total hierarchy of segments is not relevant to most situations. An anthropologist may construct a complex diagram from the replies to a large number of questions from many informants, but this is not really in the mind of any Chimbu. I collected lists of subgroups within many Chimbu tribes. Men who were not members but claimed some knowledge of the internal structure of a tribe often could enumerate the names of some subgroups, but subsequent checking with members of the tribes concerned showed this to be a conglomerate of clans, sections and subclans, without any indication of segmentary structure. Members of the tribe usually distinguished the groups I call clans from those I call subclans, but informants within the tribe did not always completely agree upon this three-level segmentary hierarchy.

The Chimbu ideology of group structure is agnatic — they call their main groups 'father-son' *(nem-angigl)*. A very wide group which I call a phratry is composed of several of the groups I call clans. This is expressed as a set of brothers, not always with an inclusive name for the father of them all. Clan names are taken from the founder's name with a suffix meaning 'line' or 'rope.' The phratry need not have any corporate property or functions, but when several clans which are associated as all or part of a phratry are in addition localized, they usually have a territorial block and form all or part of a tribe. Many such subtribes have a tradition of recent fission from a single exogamous clan.

Different informants in the same tribe often give different versions of phratry composition. There is substantial agreement about the 'brotherhood' of the several founders of clans now associated in a tribe or subtribe, but connections to those outside may vary. Thus all our informants in Naregu tribe named the three clans Pentagu, Numambugu and Kombaku as 'brothers.' But their conception of the relation of Naregu to Siku and Kombuku, now some miles away, and Gamgani, now a small group mostly attached to one subclan of Numambugu, differed.

Clans are segmented in a number of ways. Often there is a division into two sections and within each section certain groups are closely associated as pairs whose names are often linked, for example, Bau-Aundugu. However, the more or less fixed named groups which I call subclans are regularly identified as 'brother' groups. Thus the Chimbu's general model ignores the clan sections and subclan linkages and identifies phratry, clan and subclan, the main named groups.

The Chimbu segmentary system takes the form of a patrilineal mechanical model: the segments are viewed as having the nesting characteristics of a unilineal descent system. A set of 'son' groups is said to be descended from one of a set of 'brothers.' But there is not always agreement about the founder or 'father' of these 'brothers.' In Chimbu this series does not have many clear levels and some groupings which can be observed in action and in reference are not depicted as levels of the descent model. Nevertheless, the Chimbu model of their structure has many characteristics of a lineage system.

The clan, with an average population of 600-700, is the usual unit of exogamy. Chimbu state of some groups that they were formerly parts of an exogamous group and have only in the past one or two generations begun to allow marriage between the segments. In these cases, as with other exogamous groups, each present exogamous group is named as a 'brother' of the others — the clans as viewed today are parallel. Chimbu are unconcerned about questions of past relationships of segments, and do not attempt to systematize their accounts of the structure. In different contexts a different level of segmentation may be relevant — consistency is not sought for the system as a whole. Brother clans in a local phratry, tribe or subtribe are bound to one another by many ties of kinship and affinity. They make prestations to one other. Within the clan, joint action in fights and in prestations is often taken by clan sections and linked pairs of subclans. These may also cooperate in local enterprises such as erecting fences. Such activities are mainly cooperative works for local residents, done often in the name of groups. Subclans are more common activity units. They are the main organizing units at marriages and funerals, and undertake some joint agricultural activities.

The patrilineal segmentary model is not consistently carried within the subclan. The resident population of a subclan group varies from about 50 to 250, composed of 15-60 men and their families. The major divisions of subclans are irregular. Chimbu are reluctant to admit that the subclan is internally subdivided and the subgrouping may shift from time to time, on different ceremonial occasions, or for local activities. In some groups a division is attributed to a past quarrel after which subgroups use different cemeteries or ceremonial grounds. Divisions are not clear-cut. Residence in men's houses, neighborhood, farming cooperation and contributions to prestations may cut a subclan differently. Some subclan section land blocks are discernible and expressed in men's house groupings (Brookfield and Brown 1963). Chimbu refer to the subclan section as a men's house or 'one blood' *(boromai suara)*. It is conceived as a group of close agnates or lineage mates and is relevant in fixing the prohibition on marrying into the mother's 'one blood' group. The concept includes lineage, locality, men's house, cemetery, ceremonial ground, and following of a big man, but these criteria do not in practice all include the same men.

Most of the members of the 'one blood' groups in the Mintima area could be organized on an inclusive genealogy of some sort known to a few old men in the group. When these genealogies were given, they were not usually connected to the clan-subclan father-son tie. Rather, the 'one blood' group began with a subclan section founder and named his sons, carrying the genealogy through males and occasionally wives down to living men in a number of generations. These varied in size from 12 to 40 men and in the form of the lineage. One group was said to be descended from one man with four 'wives,' with living men as his grandsons; another listed seven 'brothers,' whose sons and grandsons are now adult men; and still another consisted of a founder, four 'sons' who are now old men and their sons. A more lineage-like form of three to seven generations was given for other groups. In these genealogies, many inconsistencies and confusions appeared, and the Chimbu custom of naming boys after their fathers' fathers or fathers' brothers contributes to this.

As recited, these were all patrilineages with no non-agnatic branches. They did not contain any men who were not patrilineal descendants. But the groups all had as resident and active members men who were not mentioned in the genealogy. Only further inquiry could link these men to the genealogies and some discrepancies were never cleared up. There were many cases when a man was, as far as I could determine, a fully accepted member of the group, yet not listed in the lineage. Such men were often either the son of a man who had lived uxorilocally (in his wife's patrilineal group) or had been adopted in childhood as an orphan or the son of a divorcée, most often by his mother's brother, but sometimes by another kinsman or affine. Such men were related to the patrilineal group as sons of female members, or occasionally sons' sons of female members. However, there were some other relations, such as that of wife's brother or wife's sister's son, linking such a man to the group. Accretion is not masked by fictional agnation. A man becomes a participating member of a group in which he resides as a husband or as a woman's son, or another non-agnatic kinsman or affine. The descendants of females who have become so affiliated, and of others, are classed as members. Several men who have long lived in the Mintima groups, but whose fathers were known to be born members of other groups were prominent leaders.

In other 'one blood' groups, no general genealogy was known, the only traceable genealogical ties being from the living to their parents or grandparents and some collateral relatives. A large proportion of the living members of the group could be identified by their ties in these small genealogies and the majority of the male members of these groups were said to be linked by descent through a line of males.

Throughout, among the men patrilineally related to resident members are some who have lived elsewhere closely associated with their matrilateral kin or affines for many years. Most of these men are well known to their agnatic relatives and visit or meet now and then. They often attend funerals and contribute to marriage payments. But if they live farther than about two miles from the center of subclan settlement, they rarely use land agnatically inherited. In only a few cases, where some land was not much more than a mile from the man's home, was any land used for gardens or houses. We also know many men who are natal members of groups elsewhere and live temporarily or permanently in the Mintima area. The same situation holds; they occasionally visit their agnates but rarely use land. The other criteria for 'one blood' group — men's houses, participation in the ceremonial activities, burial in a cemetery, and following one leader — do not often fall together to include the same men.

Individual movement follows marriage patterns. Most marriage takes place within the tribe (44%) and in neighboring tribes (46%). Matrilateral kin and affines are mostly within about four miles of a man's home (Brown 1964). Visits and even long residence with matrilateral kin or affines rarely take a man out of reach of his own subclan. Quarrels or accusations of sorcery often force a temporary move. In the past, defeat in fighting made some individuals and families seek refuge with more distant relatives, and in recent years the development of cash crops, especially coffee which grows only in the lower altitudes of Chimbu, has brought some movement. We know a number of men who have their own and their wives' houses on land of their non-agnatic kin or affines but maintain close ties with their own agnates and participate in all their activities, and a few men who have become estranged from their agnates, retain some of their natal land and spend most of their time with kinsmen in nearby clans.

There are a number of common circumstances of movement. Illness, fear of sorcery or accusation of sorcery might make a woman take her children and leave her husband's group to live in her own with her father or brother. She is given garden and house land. If this move leads to divorce or brings her husband to dwell uxorilocally, it might be prolonged so that the children are regarded as members of their mother's group. Widows also bring their children home quite often. A leading man attracts followers, most often his wives' brothers and daughters' husbands. They are given land and help in their payments and often remain in the adoptive group. Leading men may also take in widows and other women as additional wives, adding dependents and building up a following in this manner. People regard the main contribution to a man's marriage payment as defining the man's group membership. Thus, when a non-agnate who lives with the adoptive group is given the bulk of his marriage payment by that group, they consider him a member. They do not expect him later to return to his agnates, but I have seen this happen in a number of cases.

A tribe is a different sort of group from these quasi-descent units. It combines descent with alliance, and some tribes are also phratries with a tradition of common descent and segmentation from a single clan to several intermarrying clans. Most tribes are alliances between such parts of phratries. Many of them have double names, such as Siambuga-Wauga. Tribal territories vary greatly in size, but the majority are 5-10 square miles, with a population numbering 1,000-4,000. They form units for war and ceremony, and these are highly-valued activities which bring esteem to the tribe and its members. Tribal pride is based upon performance in war and ceremony, skill, wealth and display. The tribe is the only Chimbu unit which has a clear-cut exclusive and discrete territory. Nearly all clans and smaller units consist of scattered plots within the larger tribal territory. Thus, whenever a tribal boundary is attacked, the land of several segments is in danger. The tribe is thus the most natural unit for fighting and defense.

Traditionally, the tribe is the largest named unit. Only at a distance are groups and tribes referred to by a directional term meaning those to the west or east, or in the higher ranges, or by regional name, referring to a river or mountain. Rivalry in ceremony and fighting characterize inter-tribal relations. Fear of sorcery and poison from long-term enemies prevents exchange and feasts. Then there are some intertribal boundaries which are social barriers and battlegrounds.

Although the general outline of group structure resembles a segmentary lineage form, the Chimbu do not think of it as hierarchical and expanding; they only use the 'father-son-brother' image to describe relations within a level or between two levels. Over time, the expanding population pressed upon land resources, made agriculture more intensive, reallocated local land, fought and migrated to less densely settled areas. Clans grew; some divided and continued in the area so that local phratries remained as the basis of a tribe; others broke apart, one section migrating and joining a different tribe. Tribal traditions were not forced to conform to a segmentary lineage model. Rather, the multiplicity of traditions and complexity of relations cannot be drawn into a single model, even within a tribe. People in other tribes may know the names of segments but not their relations of inclusion or separation.

Chapter 8

Big Men and Small

STATUS DIFFERENCES among Chimbu youths are hardly discernible except perhaps as they may vary in their intelligence, ambition, or skill in singing and dancing and success with girls. A youth, even if he earns some of his marriage costs, is heavily in debt to his kinsmen after his marriage, and in order to gain status in the traditional system, he and his wife must work hard for several years to provide vegetable food and pigs for prestations and to enter into exchanges of valuables.

While land is limited in Chimbu, every man can acquire by inheritance, loan or gift as much as his household can use — it is his own energy and ambition that really determine his achievement. The Chimbu have no ranking system for men but recognize as the lowest status 'rubbish' men or 'nothing' (yogo) men — most of whom have failed to keep a wife, but in any case they produce little and take only a small, if any, part in exchanges or distributions. Many are attached dependents of big men or of their kinsmen, and have no independent household. No more than 10% of the men would be so classified. The majority of men produce adequately for their family needs and meet their obligations in exchanges and distributions — I call these 'ordinary' men. The category includes young married men, who may later become prominent, old men who were formerly prominent but are now less active, and the majority of married men between 30 and 50, the prime age of Chimbu leaders.

Perhaps two status levels above these can be distinguished. The first I shall call 'prominent' men: they are more active and more productive than the average, initiate new gardening work, house building, fencing and such local activities, speak up in discussions, make speeches in subclan affairs and often have some dependents and followers attached to their household. Such men might have two or more wives. Perhaps 20% of the men are 'prominent.' Few men become prominent before they are thirty, and a man can hardly maintain his prominence if he has only one wife and no other attached persons. Prominent men over fifty usually have their sons, daughters and daughters' husbands, wives' younger brothers and their wives, or other attached younger families to contribute food and labor to their enterprises.

Chimbu do not make a clear and consistent distinction between this status and a higher one. They may call any prominent man a big man (*yomba pondo*), especially if he is in the speaker's own group. However, it seems more in keeping with Chimbu behavior to distinguish a status of big man as those, perhaps 5%, one or two in each subclan, who are more than prominent, who make speeches at their clan prestations and meetings when the main organizers are of a different subclan, who speak at tribal ceremonies, initiate important tribal and clan enterprises and whose disapproval is likely to stop any plan from being carried out. Big men are the largest participants in all exchange relationships: they engage in more frequent transactions than other men, and their ties extend to more distant tribes. In recent years, the big men have often been *luluais*, local government councillors, large coffee producers with employees, and owners of shops or other enterprises with a group of partially dependent followers attached to their households.

In all small groups, joint tasks are somehow accomplished and some leaders can be discerned. Chimbu often speak of men's house heads, more or less equating the men's house group with a 'one blood' group. The men's house is ideally a permanent group occupying a traditional site which serves as a center for gardening, minor ceremonies and defense against raids. But during my period of fieldwork, this did not hold and I doubt if it ever had. All the large houses have some residents who are not members of the 'one blood' group — both kin and affines of members and members of other clan segments. Hardly half of the men's houses in the Mintima area in 1958-65 were headed by prominent men, or indeed had heads at all. Some houses were the residences of two or three men of ordinary status and also a few younger men and boys, and some had only two or three men and youths. There are also houses occupied by only one man and some boys, frequently his sons.

Sometimes the impetus for building a men's house comes from one man who brings together some members of his 'one blood' group and some personal followers to construct the house. A house does not keep its exact occupancy group through its lifetime of perhaps four to nine years, but commonly has a core of men who work together on domestic tasks, contribute when payments are to be made and are most active at marriages and funerals of the group. Such groups vary considerably in size and also fluctuate in size all the time. Men tend to be attached to a single men's house, but when it is convenient, they sleep elsewhere. When their local interests change they may become attached to another house. In Chimbu some men live apart from a men's group and rarely participate in its activities, while some of the important leaders keep separate establishments. During the eight years of my study there, there was an almost complete turnover of houses but many were rebuilt on the same sites. The pig feast men's houses are usually identified with an entire subclan.

Whether or not the men's house group has a leader, several men are prominent in each subclan and most 'one blood' groups have one or two such men. Small group leadership has at different times had a different place in the larger activities of Chimbu. To some extent, different abilities have been required of leaders.

In the days before Australian administration, the daring fighter was much admired although he did not always gain a following. He was rather of a type called 'hard' by Read (1959. See also Lowman-Vayda 1968). This was a bold man, quick to anger and attack. He bragged, threatened, intimidated, assassinated unwary men, women and children and was ever eager to lead a raid against people, pigs and property of other groups. When many other men in his group wanted to attack or avenge a killing, such a man became a leader. But this was not a lasting position. Some former warriors became native officials, but on the whole their interests were inimical to the Australian administration. In 1959, after he had retired as *tultul*, one former fighting leader told me, regretfully, "Chimbu men used to be strong fighters before the white man came, but now they are like women and children." Some former warriors sufficiently changed their aims and manner of leadership to serve satisfactorily as native officials.

The more popular leader is a 'manager' or 'director' (as described by Read 1959, Reay 1964, Salisbury 1964, Strathern 1966, Brandewie 1971). His style might sometimes resemble that of the bold warrior, as it was an essential part of his pose to demand respect for the group he represented. Beyond his own small group he is highly regarded as a man of wealth, oratory and judgment. He succeeds in gaining widespread support for the enterprises he urges as a result of taking up popular causes, wise timing of activities to support, or wise choice of occasion. The large-scale feasts of Chimbu can be carried out only under favorable conditions for expanded gardening, pig raising and pandanus ripening. Coordination is essential. The clan's and tribe's reputation rest on the showing they make in these festivities. A successful group is also strong and coordinated enough to withstand attacks from other tribes. Occasionally intertribal fighting dissipates all this and the tribe breaks up. Sections migrate and form new alliances. Successful leadership keeps the tribe together to make an impressive display and prestation and to withstand attacks.

These conditions did not bring about any permanent leaders. The individual leaders can lose their following as they age and are unable to keep up their activities or fail in any enterprise. There is no accumulation of property or inheritance and little opportunity to provide for descendants. Land is inherited, but additional land can be acquired, and inherited land can be lost if rights are not defended. Personal pride is asserted when men claim that their fathers had been big men, but in fact I saw little continuity of leadership.

There is not yet much evidence of succession or continuity of prestige or privilege, but as economic opportunities and differential property holding develop, status differentiation may be inherited.

Chapter 9

Cycles and Transactions

MANY OF THE activities of Chimbu — the use of garden land, feasts, exchanges, and other transactions are fluctuating or cyclical. Indeed, it is most difficult to distinguish the dynamic fluctuations of daily life and those which depend on a cycle or some combination or intersection of cycles. We have seen how a young man reaches maturity, extending his relationships and transactions to a wide range of people. The crucial event in his life is not his initiation, but rather his marriage and the complex of ties which derive from affinal links. Debts are paid in relations with kinsmen and affines, are adjusted and resolved by an exchange of goods.

The segmentary model of Chimbu society suggests an expanding and segmenting social group, a long-term growth over time. In the course of this, either the scale of activities is extended, so that once-small gifts are now interclan exchanges, or a periodic revision of activities is made in accordance with the new scale of groups. We were told some traditions which suggest that exogamous units have divided and permit marriages between former segments. However, we have no firm data on the rate of expansion of these groups, or the processes of segmentation. Vegetable feasts may be given between clans, subtribes or tribes — they are not definitive of a particular level of intergroup relations. Chimbu, with the greatest density of population in New Guinea, also has the largest clan, subtribe and tribal groups.

The basic economic group is normally the individual family household. In polygynous families, each wife with her children has an independent household: a separate house, gardens and pigs. The husband is active in each wife's household and maintains rights over land, pigs and crops. Between households, there are various levels of cooperation for different sorts of activities. Mutual aid and assistance between kinsmen and between the neighboring families of men in the men's house are ordinary and commonplace. Whenever there is a gathering, or visitors at the men's house, several of the women join together to provide food. This small-scale sharing of food does not make heavy demands on normal food requirements of a family. It is a matter of each woman digging up a few extra pounds of sweet potatoes from a plot which is currently ready for harvesting. Each family allows for such minor additional supplies as are used in small distributions outside the household. Men grow bananas and sugar cane in order to provide these for occasional refreshment to friends and helpers and for festive distributions. Some plants, such as peanuts, taro and yams, are often used for such festive occasions. No seasonal harvest is involved in these plants; they are ready at almost any time of the year.

The large-scale food production and feasts of the Chimbu have both an individual and a group aspect. Each man is an independent householder in a number of different sorts of reciprocal relations with men of his subclan and clan and also in exchange relations with persons outside his clan who are his non-agnatic kinsmen and affines. The tribe is a unit for some large ceremonial food distributions, but also segments of the tribe are units for certain sorts of production, display and exchange activities.

Within the clan, different sorts of relationship exist, as in any segmentary system. There is no definitive segment which is the cooperative and sharing group. A close group of agnates is intensely involved in mutual aid and support in all activities. The men of a subclan section may work together in fencing, house building and garden preparation, and provide a large part of the marriage or death payments required by one of their number. The whole subclan is less often called together, but its members do contribute to large tasks and important payments. Members of other subclans within the clan rarely participate unless their land or interests are involved, or they are personally friendly and help to provide goods for a marriage or death payment. The clan is the largest group within which such assistance is given. Relationships of mutual aid in work and in financial support outside the clan are mainly between affines and matrilateral kin. Some such relationship also exists within the clan when men are related, as, for example, the sons of sisters.

Special vegetable distributions (*mogena biri*) are held periodically. They are collaborative affairs of a clan, subtribe or tribe and are presented to another clan, to a subtribe within or outside the tribe, or intertribally. Usually these center around some special festive food, of which the most important are pandanus nuts and oil fruits. Not all tribes, or all men, have rights to both types of pandanus. These tree products are not only seasonal but rather unpredictably produced in large quantity only every few years. When a large nut crop is observed to be developing, some men build houses near the groves to guard their trees. They may then plan a large distribution, and plant extra areas with food crops for it. The prestation includes marsupials, chickens, bananas, sugar cane, sweet potatoes, taro, yams, other vegetables, and many special foods, some now purchased in local shops. The donors may have some products not available in the recipients' area, because of altitude or other special circumstances. A clan, or subtribe, plans together. Small-scale group distributions may be given more than once a year, but the large pandanus nut or oil fruit distributions occur only at intervals of several years.

At a tribal vegetable distribution, a huge pile, 20-50 yards in diameter, and piled high in some sections, is made up by the produce contributed by the many participants. The invited guests dance, as do the hosts. Speeches are made pointing out the relations between the two groups. Then the whole pile is dismantled, parcel by parcel, and each is designated by an individual donor for an individual recipient.

Vegetable feasts are thus group displays and individual gifts, made by each man to his exchange partners on these group-organized occasions. *Mogena biri* between tribes should alternate every few years. A long delay in returning a vegetable distribution is loudly criticized by the creditor tribe and the debtors lose in prestige. This further contributes to feelings of hostility from other causes, such as quarrels over marriages and land. Intergroup relations and prestige revolve about displays of strength and wealth in fighting and feasts.

There are a few occasions in which a person or a group of people such as a tribe, clan or clan segment puts together vegetable food, pigs and valuables, as in a *mogena biri,* to provide payment to another person or group. These are often an aftermath of conflict or warfare, and the particular payment might be compensation to allies, compensation for injury, truce payments, thanks payments for help or hospitality. Such payments may create or re-establish an intergroup relationship which is followed by intermarriage.

The pig ceremony (*bugla gende*) is the largest collective activity of a Chimbu tribe, requiring the cooperation of several hundred men to provide food and pigs, build houses and dance over a period of many months. We estimate that a Chimbu tribe may hold a pig ceremony every six to ten years. The time from the end of one pig feast to the first stages of the following one may vary greatly, but I do not think it could be less than three years. Compared to pig ceremonies of the Eastern Highlands, the Chimbu feast is a much larger affair, in the number of participants and the quantity of food and pigs. A Chimbu tribe kills about as many pigs as it has people. Usually several tribes prepare for and hold the pig feast more or less simultaneously, but coordination of activities is only within a tribe. There are two main sets of tribes, which have alternated their feasts. Many factors may affect the frequency of these feasts. In the past, in times of tribal warfare, the additional effort of food growing for pig raising and guests may not have been possible. Individual tribes do not join with the others of their set if they feel they cannot make an adequate showing. Thus the interval between successive feasts is not regular, and a tribe or sub-tribe may delay its feast. Since former pig gifts received should be recipro-cated, they remain in debt and lose prestige when they fail to hold a feast. More recently some groups have delayed or stopped holding their pig cere-monies because other activities, particularly economic development in coffee, have diverted their interests. In 1963 a preparatory announcement was made in one Naregu clan nine years after the last feast, and there has been further delay to make an interval of sixteen years.

The whole tribe, under the direction of its big men, must agree that its pigs are large and numerous enough to begin to prepare for a feast. Each separate group, normally a subclan, holds a small preparatory celebration in which cooked food including pigs is shared. Bamboo flutes are played to announce the intention of the group to hold the feast. Flutes may be first shown ceremonially to small boys at this time. Boys' initiation is no longer carried out in central Chimbu, and flutes no longer are sacred objects associated with birds and spirits, concealed from women and chil-dren. However, pairs of bamboo flutes, each named and tuned to a par-ticular pitch, are still kept by subclans, subclan sections or smaller family groups and played by men during the pig feast preparations.

After this preparatory phase, the tribe's efforts are directed toward increasing and fattening their pigs. In another year or two, when they are nearing sufficiency — that is over two thousand full-grown pigs — the ceremonial grounds are set up. Each ceremonial ground, large or small, has much the same ground plan. The central spot is reserved for the *bolum* (sacred pig house), and men's houses, normally one for each subclan, sur-round the central spot. The distinctive architectural features of ceremonial grounds are very long houses which are used as shelters for the families of the men giving the pig ceremony and for visitors. For a short period at the climax of the pig ceremony, several thousand people, with pigs, personal goods, food and firewood are all gathered in or near these buildings. A single subclan builds one, two or more of these long houses which extend for a hundred yards or more, wherever there is relatively level ground.

After the houses are completed new fires are kindled, and many weeks, often months, of dancing follow. Every few days, groups of dancers visit ceremonial grounds of their own and other tribes in the area, and groups from neighboring tribes, who are not holding a pig feast at the same time, come to dance at the ceremonial grounds. The dancers are chiefly young men, but most dancing groups also include a few of the unmarried girls of the clan; the men sing, the girls only dance. Both carry drums or weapons such as bows and arrow, spear or axe, and wear on their heads a display of wealth in feathers and plumes, and the wigs and decorated *gerua* (headboards) of ritual importance. Wealth and strength are thus joined together. Towards the end of the dancing period, the group which is holding the ceremony gives some special dance performances which are symbolic of myths or historical events, such as the origins of sacred ferns, animals, plants, etc. The right to dance certain symbolic movements is restricted to men in those segments traditionally associated with the dance. The songs, which commemorate events and refer to plants, animals, birds, courtship, weather conditions and group relations are rehearsed by the men of the clan and then sung publicly for all to hear. New songs are composed from time to time to commemorate recent events.

Towards the climax of the pig ceremony, the central *bolum* is built secretly at night by men, and smeared with pig blood and fat to ward off sickness and death. The jaws of the first or 'spirit' pigs (*gigl kambu*) are hung on the *bolum* to indicate the number of pigs killed by the group. Distribution of the 'spirit meat' is mainly within the tribe and very frequently to friends and close associates within the subclan. But at this time there are also some collective prestations to groups for a debt, or to establish friendly relations, as at a *mogena biri*. Marriages are often made at this time, and the valuables and cooked pigs exchanged at the ceremonial ground. Death payments and other compensation to individuals or groups are made with *gigl kambu*.

The climax of the *bugla gende* is a mock attack on the ceremonial ground by male dancers and a fertility ritual which involves blessing sweet potato vines, women and pigs. Pigs are killed in a cemetery (which usually adjoins the ceremonial ground) as a sacrifice to the ancestors. They are then carried into the central ceremonial area and lined up so that each group's pigs can be displayed. Afterwards, all the pigs are taken back by their owners, cooked with the help of friends and relatives in other tribes who are not occupied with their own pig feast and finally distributed. Very commonly, the people who help in cooking the pigs are the recipients of the pigs. The final distribution consists of whole pigs or half-sides of pigs. Pigs are not cut up into small portions as they are at other feasts. The number of pigs killed and distributed varies — from two or three by the poorest man to five to seven killed by some wealthy big men, in the first distribution, and ten to twelve in the second distribution.

The pig ceremony is the high point of Chimbu tribal collaboration, display and prestige. All the members are decorated with feathers, shells and other finery and they display the pride of the tribe: their young men, their young girls, their valuables and their productive capacity in the quantity of pork which they can give away. It demonstrates the strength and wealth of the tribe to visitors, observers and recipients from all other tribes.

An exchange involving the giving and receiving of foodstuffs, pigs and/or valuables may be interpersonal from a man to his brother-in-law, but most exchanges are in fact and in concept intergroup. The fulcrum of the majority of exchanges is marriage — the marriage payment, birth and death payments, and all intergroup feasts are between affines or kin in different clans who are related as cross-cousins. Thus, when a tribe presents pandanus nuts to a neighboring tribe, the actual gifts are from a man to his brother-in-law, mother's brother, sister's son, or similar sort of relative, a result of the system of exogamy.

Although much of Chimbu activity and planning is guided by cycles of family development, land use and large ceremonies, none of these is on any fixed time scale, and the interplay between these cycles is highly complex. Thus food production must increase in preparation for a large feast. The location of ceremonial grounds, pig herds and gardens should minimize the carrying distances, and yet the cultivation and fallow land use and cycle may make this very difficult for some families. A feast may occur when marriage or death payments are needed, sometimes unpredictably. Thus the allocation of pigs and valuables must adapt to particular family requirements.

Chapter 10

Strife

STRIFE CHARACTERIZES Chimbu life. It was until recently expressed in frequent fights and warfare, uncontrolled by any authority. Today, the colonial administration usually succeeds in stopping fights before they develop into interclan or intertribal warfare. The fighters are sent to jail for a few months.

The ecological situation of Chimbu fits its flexibility in group structure and struggle for land. The territorial units are blocks of land held by tribes or subtribes — several square miles including arable land suitable for a variety of crops, bushland with some useful natural products, and some pig forage land. A few tribes are short of forest, nut pandanus, or some other desired product. Within the tribe or subtribe, the scarce and desired land types are divided among clans, subclans and individuals, so that most persons have access to every available land type. This allocation of resources results in fragmentation of land holdings between individuals and subgroups. The territory of members of a subclan consists of a number of patches of land, or strips extending up and down slopes. This territorial complexity produces a profusion of intergroup boundaries over which quarrels are common due to encroachment, the intrusion of pigs, pig theft, disagreement about boundaries, etc.

In addition to a premium on certain types of land, there is a general shortage of land, and especially of good arable land: in parts of the Chimbu area densities reach 500 per square mile. The perennial shortage of high-protein foods, pigs and nuts, is alleviated, when possible, by theft — a common cause of war. Intertribal fights and raids destroyed crops, livestock

51

and houses, thus intensifying shortages and competition for land and resources.

Chimbu is the most densely populated area in New Guinea, and these
pressures are especially high. But many other New Guinea communities,
particularly in the highlands, are reported to have also been in a constant
state of hostility with neighbors, and tribal warfare is frequent. The same
pattern of fighting occurs in the densely and in the sparsely populated
areas of Chimbu, so that the tension cannot be attributed to land shortage
alone.

Intergroup strife seems to be endemic to New Guinea highland societies.
It is accompanied by an absence of authoritative controls. Chimbu children are relatively unrestricted. Girls may be in charge of smaller children,
but boys have no regular tasks, and do little garden work until adulthood.
They rarely have their own gardens before marriage, at about 20. Adoles-
cents spend many of their nights at courting parties, their days resting or
strolling about. Hard work does not begin until after marriage. Then the
girls are taken to a strange community where they may be, for the first
time in their lives, beaten for laziness. Even after marriage the men are not
subject to control by their elders or leaders — they are free to work, fight,
visit or rest, with only their ambition, the pressure of group opinion and
obligations to direct their activities.

Excessive interpersonal problems, disputes or sorcery accusations in a
family's home area can be avoided by a temporary or permanent removal
to a distant part of the subclan territory or to relatives outside the clan —
a man's mother's relatives or married sister's husband, or a wife's parents or
brothers. These relatives would offer hospitality, house room and land,
and many visits are extended to permanent immigration and adoption
into the segment and clan of the host. Thus the obligation of mutual aid
to patrilineal kinsmen is not totally binding and inescapable — a man can
take his family to other relatives and be welcome, long-term guests.

Strife between husband and wife in the early months of marriage quite
often results in separation, sometimes in permanent divorce. After children
are born, the dissolution of a family is less common, since the children are
claimed by the father and the wife might lose them if she leaves the husband. When the wife is widowed, ill or accused of sorcery, she sometimes
takes the children to her paternal home; this may be a permanent move
for all of them, but some dispute over the allegiance of children is likely
to follow. Chimbu plays and pantomines, *gitn darkwa*, portray quarrels,
fights, battles, magic and curing. These matters of tension, danger, and
conflict are acted out vigorously to provide entertainment to all.

There are no centralized mystical sanctions or controls, and no organized
propitiation or worship. The pig feast has as a general aim group welfare

and fertility. Pigs are killed in cemeteries and cooked at ceremonial grounds because this pleases the ancestors and contributes to the welfare of the living.

Supernatural dangers are avoided, when possible, by the Chimbu. There are spirits, ghosts and sites where various kinds of evil influences are thought to lurk. People avoid such areas, and few are willing to travel alone at night. But their notions about sorcery and witchcraft are extremely hazy. After a death, especially the death of a young person, sorcery is often blamed, and there is sometimes an attempt to discover the sorcerer. When public opinion is aroused, an accused sorcerer may be forced to leave the group or locality for a time and reside elsewhere. This is most common with the wives of men in the local group. Both the wife and her husband may reside for a time with her relatives as a result of such accusation. When there has been a considerable amount of illness and death in a group, some people may move away in order to escape what they believe to be evil influences, whether these are spirits or sorcerers or unknown influences. All of these practices lead to a general air of uncertainty, insecurity, secretiveness and avoidance of strangers. Earlier observers report magic and divination to determine the cause of illness and death. These are even more secretive now that strangers are so frequently there.

There are no governmental officials of any kind, certainly no persons charged with the maintenance of law and order, or to whom respect is owed by reason of rank or status. The big men become leaders through their own energies and ambitions in domestic activities, group activities, warfare and ceremony. They propose enterprises and attract followers, but they cannot punish those who fail to follow. They can only influence their fellows to join in a fight, or make up a display or ceremony.

There is no way to impose group loyalty, and there are many avenues of escape and avoidance of social pressures. Men mostly reside and participate as members of their fathers' locality and subclan, but non-agnatic kin and affines offer alternative places of residence, gardens and affiliation. These provide sanctuary in war, an escape from quarrels and boredom. Permanent moves to join non-agnates are fairly common, and the guest suffers little disadvantage in a adoptive group. If, however, he makes trouble as a guest he may be pressed to leave. He cannot be deprived of his land in his natal group and if he cannot get along with fellow-members of his subclan he may live apart, within the area. But there is no security or protection among strangers. People only venture outside their own tribal areas in the company of friendly hosts — kinsmen or exchange partners. Long trading trips are undertaken through a chain of friends.

All of this suggests a very great deal of individual freedom, an absence of organized social control. Yet Chimbu is not a society of independent, isolated families. Group activities are common — ceremonies, meetings, collaborative working parties are frequent and the men rarely work alone.

These group activities bring together members of the smaller segments and these less frequently combine in larger enterprises. The scattered pattern of land holdings gives members of different segments a common interest — in maintaining a fence, clearing a fallow area, building houses, defending their holdings against intruders.

There is also group pride and prestige in periodic ceremonies — which include the distribution of produce — a tribe, or, sometimes, a clan, displays its strength, wealth and productive ability. Planning and organization are essential to the success of such distributions, and the reward is admiration and the expectation of a return in the future. The distributions are at the same time the occasions for honoring individual obligations, each man is enmeshed in exchange relationships with his non-agnatic kin and affines in other groups which are the basis of the circulation of valued goods, produce and women. In supporting tribal ceremonies, a man repays debts, enlarges his extra-tribal connections, and enhances his personal standing within and outside the tribe. At the same time, the ceremonies express inter-tribal competition.

Support of the group in its external relations has another, essential benefit to the individual. His property is dispersed in several parts of tribal territory, and he can call upon his clansmen, kin and affines within the tribe for additional land if he has not inherited sufficient for his needs. He has a great interest in maintaining and increasing the tribal holding. An attack on any part of tribal territory is a danger to him, and he joins his group to defend itself against such attacks as a member of a tribal army. He also has real or potential land interests in the territory of other tribes with which he has a matrilateral or affinal tie; these bring him to support these groups against outside attack. He may refuse to support an attack by his tribe on one of these, but unless he is currently using land there or dwelling there, his loyalties are primarily to his own tribe. Very few men divide their interests between two tribes for any period of time; an immigrant of long residence in another tribe is expected to support it in its conflicts, even against his natal tribe. Within the tribe, maintenance of double allegiance and land interests in two clans, own and maternal or affinal, is less likely to divide loyalties — prolonged violent conflict within the tribe is rare.

Within smaller segments, a man is in an intensive relationship of mutual aid and dependence. It is possible to independently carry out most domestic activities, but few men do this, and the occasional need for goods to make essential payments, at marriage or death, requires the collaboration of men in a subclan or other segment. Cooperation at this level is a combination of preference and necessity; every man is partly autonomous and more or less constantly helping others or being helped by others. His interaction is not determined by coercion or authority, but by personal choice and advantage. He also helps and is helped by his own friends and relatives outside his group. As Malinowski said of the Trobriands: "The configuration of obligations . . . makes it impossible for the native to shirk his responsibilities without suffering for it in the future." (1926:59).

In Chimbu, quarrels and disputes are frequent, and solutions are rare. Fights were common not only between the larger groups — the tribes — but between clans within the tribe and locally between subclans of these clans. Large fights could arise over trivial quarrels, and no authority could control or punish the offenders. Even within the local group there was no maintenance of law and order by headmen who could settle disputes and prevent violence, and there was no regular social unit which was the usual military force against outside aggressors. It was never possible to be certain whether a dispute would provoke a destructive war or be received with the exchange of valuables and friendly relations. Long-term accounts of intergroup relations frequently showed that there were periods of enmity in which any dispute might lead to a large fight, and other periods of alliance in which disputes were solved by exchanges, friendly relations and intermarriage.

This competitive, individualistic society does not offer regular and reliable support for the individual in his personal conflicts. The group is concerned with its property in land and its reputation. Nearly all members combine to defend these. The members are so identified that in an intergroup conflict all members are involved; vengeance might be taken against any of them, and interpersonal disputes are seen as conflicts between the groups which the protagonists represent. Forces are mobilized through opposition of the largest units represented by the protagonists and their allies; fighting is an enjoyable pastime. During periods of intergroup hostility, small raids and murders of men, women and children, theft of pigs and destruction of property are common. Chimbu proudly describe their roles in sneak attacks. Daring and provocative acts, thefts and assaults were common incidents between tribes, and not rare between clans within a tribe. Any strangers who entered the area were thus open to attacks to obtain their goods. This was the first reaction to Australian exploring groups and missionaries.

The kinds of disputes, but perhaps not their relative frequency, can almost be predicted from Chimbu interests. Yet these are common in most societies. Quarrels over property and sexual rights prevail: children fight over possessions, young women over men, co-wives over property and privilege, men over sexual rights to women, payments, goods, animals, gardens, land and produce, and husbands and wives over goods and services. There are very few ideological quarrels, disputes over belief, procedure, precedence, insubordination, ritual infractions, treason. Chimbu assert themselves; they grasp from one another, in the tribe and outside. Grasping is not regarded as wrong, but they readily take offense at the assertion of others.

The intensity of reaction to any conflict of interests varies with the previous relations between the parties, their characters, and the relations between the groups of which they are members. Assaults and homicide are common, but these cases have a history — a man does not strike another without some sort of provocation; the quarrel is not over the injury but the conflict of interests which provoked the blow, or it may be retaliation against the group of which the victim is just one member. Once there is a serious injury or murder, the dispute is considered more serious, and vengeance is expected; at this stage a group raid or battle is likely.

Suicide, threats of violence or sorcery, and actual self-help are the traditional means of facing conflict situations, especially between groups. Within the subclan and clan, and perhaps sometimes within the tribe or even between tribes, public discussion might sometimes resolve conflicts, perhaps with payment of compensation or an exchange of goods. In reply to my question, "What would have been done about this in the old days?", the reply was always, "We would fight." The fighters were always men, asserting their own or their group's rights against an opponent. Women strike one another, or men, in anger, but they do not fight in raids or battles.

The great majority of conflicts concern property, debt, and interpersonal, intergroup relations, often involving women. A small proportion are sorcery accusations. There are a few cases of insult, spreading false rumor, and assaults under obscure circumstances. About half of the cases involve goods and property: debts, land disputes, property damage by pigs, theft, etc.; most of the remainder are sexual — marital quarrels, divorces, adultery, jealousy, remarriage of widows. These are the things that Chimbu are concerned about. The intensity of reaction to any conflict of interests varies with the previous relations between the parties, their characters, and the relations between the groups of which they are members.

Chapter 11

Warfare

ALTHOUGH IN SOME parts of the New Guinea highlands, traditionally, fighting was prohibited or quickly stopped within a clan or a local group, intraclan fights and killings occurred in Chimbu, and no authority existed for settlement. The relations between tribes were characterized by a permanent state of enmity, which was an important contributing factor to the unity of a tribe. Fighting is the source of personal prestige, the frequent result of minor dispute or theft, and a means of acquiring land. People and small groups fled from their conquerors, and this was an important source of new alliances, migrations and population redistribution.

The first European visitors to the highlands encountered intervillage and intertribal fighting wherever they went, and 35 years of administration has not eradicated it in the Chimbu area. After the establishment of a government station and prompt action taken by Australian officers to stop tribal fighting, natives often express gratitude for the new peace and security, especially as exchange has flourished in security and with the introduction of more shells and other valuable goods. Yet this is not wholeheartedly appreciated by the warriors. They often find the new life dull.

The Chimbu weapons include spears, bows and arrows and axes. The spear is eight or nine feet long, of hardwood, with three prongs about four feet from the tip, and a series of barbs tapering from the prongs to the pointed tip. In addition to being used in warfare, in close fighting, it is also carried in ceremonial processions, in dancing, and by speakers in ceremonies. It is a highly symbolic object, used by leaders in competitive activities or fighting and ceremony. Chimbu bows are made of hardwood

57

or bamboo, four or more feet long, with a strip of bamboo for the string. They are used with an arrow about four feet long, composed of a cane shaft and a carved and barbed hardwood tip or a simple bamboo point inserted in the shaft and bound on with fibers. Bows and arrows were used by fighters at some distance from one another, who backed up the group of spear fighters who led in ceremonial fight formation. The large, thin bladed, polished stone axe, with a decorated handle, known as the "Hagen" axe, which was a valuable in marriage payments, was carried hung over a man's belt and used in hand-to-hand fighting. Clubs, roughly fashioned of wood, fence posts or other sticks, were used for fighting in an emergency. The Chimbu made large, heavy shields, up to five feet high and two feet wide, of slightly curved planks of wood, with a rope-hold, decorated with paint and feathers. These were carried by the spearmen in battle, giving maximum protection but little mobility.

The mode of fighting is described by Vial, who was an officer in Chimbu in 1938-9, a few years after the first Australian post was established. He portrays the Chimbu as highly strung, high-spirited, fighting for fun or over pig theft and women who run away from their husbands, feuding, insulting one another, and arming to meet the enemy on a boundary between two groups. The battle formation he describes was not the common mode of fighting, which was raiding and brawls. Battle formation of this type is reported for some other areas of the highlands, but Vial's description is the most detailed.

In each party there are a number of men with shields and spears; the rest are bowmen. All carry axes in their belts. The shields are of wood, about five feet high and two feet wide. They are carried on a sling over the left shoulder, and are manipulated by looping the thumb through a rope down one edge. Arranged like this they can be swung to protect the back, the front, or the left side of the body. In his right hand the warrior carries a carved wooden spear with a main point and three small prongs. Bows are of palm or bamboo, and arrows are unfeathered, with hard wood or bamboo points. They are often elaborately carved.

The two parties stand on hill-tops and shout abuse and dare each other to attack. They advance towards each other, half a dozen spearmen in front, with bowmen behind. The spearmen form a line and charge the opposing half dozen spearmen, shields in front and only the right eye and ankles exposed. Behind them bowmen are waiting for a snap shot at an exposed enemy. When the spearman sees an arrow coming, he drops the edge of his shield to the ground to protect his ankles and crouches a moment until he feels the arrow hit the shield or sees it go by. That this is not always effective is proved by the number of men blind in the right eye from peering round the shield at the wrong time.

The spearman's job is to keep the enemy spearman too busy to watch arrows and to expose him to arrow fire by pulling his shield away for an instant. He does this by jabbing his spear in the shield and twisting it to one side. If he can get the opportunity, he cuts with his stone axe at the knots on the outside of the shield where the supporting ropes come through it. If the opponent is so clumsy that he exposes himself to a spear jab, that is his misfortune.

While the spearman is trying to expose or injure his opponent, the latter is trying to do the same to him, and arrows are flying from both sides.

Such skill has been evolved by the fighting natives through constant warfare that two teams of spearmen may fight for an hour or more and no one will be wounded, although innumerable arrows have been fired. The spearmen manoeuvre over a few yards of ground, rushing at each other and retreating, while the bowmen watch for openings, and, farther back, the reserves and spectators look on and shout advice. . . .

When a man is wounded, the opposing spearmen rush in for the kill. If he is down he is usually killed by a spear thrust but sometimes the bowmen get in and do the job with their axes. If he is able to retreat behind his own line of spearmen he does so, and his place is taken by another man. Only a few of the warriors of each side fight at once. Of two hundred men on one side, about six will be in the thick of the fight with their shields, sixty or seventy will be shooting arrows, and the rest will be well behind the lines watching and ready to take part if they are needed.

After several days of fighting there may be only a few flesh wounds on each side, chiefly in the legs. . . .

If no one is killed the fight may go on for days or weeks, with temporary truces when both sides feel that have had enough for the day. . . .

It looks like a game between keen players and not a matter of life and death, but there is grim reality behind it. Suppose one side has two or three men killed, is driven back, and finally flees. The victors will follow on, killing any warriors they can catch. . . .

A woman may be taken home by the man who caught her, to become one of his wives if she wishes. . . .

The people who have been forced to flee, hide themselves among the rocks of the gullies and gorges, or in deep limestone caves, taking their pigs with them if they can. . . . The victorious warriors, with their families and hundreds of natives from other groups who have no direct interest in the dispute, overrun the lands of the defeated group and destroy or carry away everything they can. Houses are burnt, bananas and bamboos are cut down, crops are destroyed, and all the goods of value that can be carried away — pigs, tame cassowaries, valuables in the houses, sweet potatoes and other foods — are taken home by whoever finds them. The plantations of casuarinas (made to supply wood for building, fencing and fuel) are burnt or ring-barked, and the trees, many years old, of the sacred groves are also killed. The destruction is thorough.[1]

It is unlikely that such large battles were frequent; the majority of killings seem to have been in small raids. One writer, a young Chimbu (Kambkama) in a semi-fictional account, gives an instance of an engagement between many thousands of troops under the discipline of experienced

[1] Leigh G. Vial, "The Fight for Fun," *Walkabout* 9, no. 1, pp. 5-9, 1942.

warriors, in a three-day battle involving tactical manoeuvres, destruction of property and thousands killed, followed by payments by the protagonist group to the opponents. This seems to me, as compared with the descriptions of my Chimbu informants and the accounts of other observers, to be a gross exaggeration of size and over-formalization of procedure.

The largest battles in the highlands are mentioned by Meggitt as Enga 'sporting fights', where two or three phratries meet on a battle ground, involving perhaps as many as 2,500 warriors, but resulting in few deaths and followed by ceremonial exchanges (1958:268). Bulmer (1960) discussing the Baiyer River area, speaks of war parties of 20-200 men. Eastern highlands clans and tribes were on the whole smaller than western, and fighting groups probably also smaller. Some of the highlands people distinguished two types of fighting: large-scale intertribal warfare and small unorganized fights or feuds where lethal weapons were not used, within the tribe or clan. A most vivid pictorial and descriptive account of Dani warfare in the highlands of West Irian is found in Gardner and Heider (1968).

Such battles were not the only, or even the main, form of fighting and warfare in Chimbu. Much more commonly, I think, there were attacks on individual persons traveling through territory of other tribes, and attacks upon houses and fields of neighboring tribes with whom there was some quarrel at the time. The Chimbu distribution of houses fits well with this form of fighting and surprise attack. The houses of women and children were rarely directly attacked, and quite often, of course, the women were members of a different tribe, perhaps that of the enemy group. But there were many attacks upon men's houses. In most of the accounts, a group came by night or just at dawn, surrounded a man's house, barred the exit door, and set fire to the house. In former days, houses that were particularly subject to such attack had escape tunnels built by the inhabitants. We heard a few stories of whole groups of men who had lived in a house being killed off in such an attack. Much more commonly, the attack was only partly successful, and a fight ensued in which the attackers were driven off. Most of the descriptions of fighting that I obtained in Chimbu were of raids, isolated killings and ambushes, rather than of battles. However, in recalling the thrilling days of the past, the story frequently ended in glory. "We drove all of the Y tribe down to the Wahgi river, where they had to take refuge with the Z tribe." Such an inclination to flee is quite common, and suggests that a high proportion of people were either non-combatants or unwilling victims in fights. Older men can cite many instances of people who fled from the enemy, and women and children who were taken to safety in another tribe. In every group today, there are men who have become incorporated after such a migration or sanctuary in warfare. This is a major cause of changes in group membership and redistribution of people.

Warfare is responsible for the fission of tribes, migration of segments, and the distribution of groups. The tribes are by no means permanent units composed of specific descent groups in a fixed territory. With the exception of some groups which hold land near Womkama in the Chimbu valley, the traditions of all groups of Chimbu state that, in a series of moves, they were forced to seek new territory as their land was occupied by conquerors. Such moves are frequently temporary, and the group may regain lost land in a later fight, or be allowed to return by the victors.

There may well have been direct competition for land as a result of population increase, but the actual quarrel which precipitates the fight is, more commonly, a fight over other kinds of property, women or pigs. The fortunes of tribes and smaller groups fluctuate. At one time, they successfully occupy conquered land and at another, they flee to unoccupied areas at the fringe of the Chimbu region. Between tribes, bitter hostilities may last for generations. Some enmities remain after tribes are separated, and an old enemy may join a war to inflict further injury to a group with which it no longer shares a common boundary.

Stories of fights are an important part of tribal traditions. They provide an explanation of group movement, present location, and intertribal relations. Even a casual inquiry in any tribe will produce some account of hostility with every neighboring tribe and some distant ones. Frequently, tribes now separated by one or more intervening tribal territories are said to have been former neighbors and one was dislodged by warfare. Local place names often refer to groups now living miles away; former ceremonial grounds and cemeteries of these evicted groups are remembered.

While all tribes fought against each of their neighbors from time to time, most of them also fought on the same side as these neighbors, at some time. Yet these were not always a genuine alliance. A group might take advantage of its enemy's diversion by a fight at some other place and attack them at a time when they are presumed to be weak. Another sort of alliance occurs when individual kinsmen or affines of the fighters join to help them in attacking an enemy. They are often members of a different tribe, although sometimes of a clan within the tribe that is not actively involved in its quarrel, and they come as friends and supporters of the main fighters against their enemy. Many of these alliances are very short-lived. If one of the helpers is injured or killed, the whole group usually retires immediately to take care of, or mourn, the casualty, and the fight may cease at that point. At some later date, when the opportunity arises, a new attack may be launched by the same or some different people. Sometimes a group is overwhelmed by the enemy group because it was unprepared or perhaps unorganized. In these cases, the defeated group would flee before the enemies, and the victors would take over the territory. A subsequent peace arrangement may allow the defeated to reoccupy some or all of this land, but in some cases, land was the basic goal of the fight, and the victors would not allow them to return. In some cases, the defeated fled to sanctuary in another group, and that group helped them to recapture their lost territory. In the general picture of a small shifting of borders within the main tribal arrangements, there were some cases of large forced migrations to new territory on the fringes of the Chimbu area requiring flight through the territory of other, at the moment, friendly groups. There were some unoccupied frontier regions only occasionally used for pig forage or gardens. Concentration of people's houses and gardens was more central in the group territory, leaving a kind of open no-man's-land between tribes with no clear tribal boundary, only this little-occupied stretch between population and garden concentrations. But the high population density and need for good agricultural land affected this distribution: some land was too valuable to leave in this way, and was strongly defended or taken and used by the victor.

TABLE I   Some Causes of Warfare in Chimbu

	Intertribal	Intratribal Between Clans	Intraclan	Total
Pig theft	2	3	3	8
Pork debt, inadequate repayment	3			3
Theft of valuables	1			1
Theft of vegetable food			2	2
Divorce	4			4
Courtship rivalry	1			1
Jealousy — husband suspected wife	1			1
Killing of young person	2			2
Death — sorcery accusation		1		1
TOTAL	14	4	5	23

In warfare, the segmentary system is only a rough predictor of alignment into opposing forces. Men join in for the pleasure of the fight, to support a fellow clansman, tribesman, kinsman or affine. My cases include some in which one subclan was allied with another tribe against its own clan and tribe. The same types of dispute, such as debts and land boundaries, can occur within the subclan or between tribes. But two quarreling subclansmen cannot muster two large opposing forces. Between subclans in a clan, disputes could become fights, usually short lived and followed by the resumption of normal intraclan relations. Members of two tribes can, in the same type of conflict, find support among their fellow tribesmen who are glad to join a fight against the other. Intertribal relations are always opposed; tribes compete in exchanges, they fight with little provocation; the links are between individual relatives and affines. Intertribal fights often include persons in other tribes in two ways — as individual supporters of the protagonists or, on a large scale, when a tribe takes advantage of the disposition of enemy forces to attack on another front.

Long-term alliances are rare, even within the tribe. If a member of a subclan is killed in battle while supporting a tribal fight, the other fighters in the subclan might drop out of the engagement. Sometimes they would turn against the subclan which was judged responsible for bringing them into the war. The segmentary pattern of alliance is fragile, and alliance often depends upon circumstances of personal conflict. All tribes are sometimes rent by internal dispute, and all tribes fight with all other tribes on their borders from time to time. The fortunes of tribes and smaller groups fluctuate; groups break off, migrate, and form new alliances.

Traditions of origin and movement of all Chimbu groups recount series of fights, migrations, reoccupations of land, fleeing from enemies, and general tribal disruption through fighting and warfare. There were many more fights and battles than there were reallocations of people on the land. Nonetheless, the land pressure was surely an important element in bringing about fighting, and over a long period of time, the movements, alliances, breaking up of tribal groups and realliances are all elements in the actual allocation of land and resources at any particular period of time. In our own area of research, several of the groups recounted quite recent flights from enemies and recent settlement on land formerly occupied sparsely by other groups. Other groups tell of the abandonment of land held undesirable for some reason, and the gift of this land to the new refugee immigrant members of the tribe. Such movements of small groups and their incorporation amongst kinsmen and in other clans provide irregularities in the segmentary system.

Yet each attack, each battle, each war has an initiating incident which is some kind of conflict between two people or between two small groups. Characteristically in Chimbu, these interpersonal disputes occur quite commonly between kinsmen and affines, and concern marriage, adultery, divorce or payments. When such a quarrel is taken up by relatives of the aggrieved parties, it may grow into a fight or a rout, or crop destruction, or the chasing of one group off its land into sanctuary elsewhere. Another major cause of conflict is some kind of quarrel over pigs. Since pigs only range between the houses in which they are kept and forage land, occasionally breaking through fences into gardens, their movements are bounded by the land of their owner and his neighbors. As population density increases, and as gardens are placed at the fringes of pig forage land, and fences deteriorate, the danger of hungry pigs invading, wandering into garden land, and of theft of pigs by neighbors who feel that they may be breaking into their land, is increased. Fights over women necessarily involve two clans, since Chimbu clans are exogamous. Thus, both conflicts, over women and pigs, are most likely to involve two groups separated from one another by a boundary or some unoccupied land, but rarely separated by another neutral group of people. The fight characteristically takes place on the land of one or the other group, or on a no man's land between them, and the aftermath of routing may well be taking over of crops and land of the defeated enemy. Thus, some redistribution of land might be an outcome of warfare.

Chimbu society was in constant flux, with individuals engaged in transaction, big men in competition, groups in rivalry for renown as producers of food and pigs, both of which depend upon land resources, and in fights over property and prestige. No rank system or form of accumulation, succession or centralization developed to overcome individual and small group competition. Although density increased and land was intensively used, permanent occupation and improvements did not occur. There was no moral or religious ideology or sanction for rank, dominance, or succession to power and wealth.

Chapter 12

The Process of Change

In 1960 THIS statement was made at a tribal discussion, translated into English and written in a record book at Wandi by some literate New Guinean:

Europeans Discovered Highlands 27 Years Ago.
1933 - 1960

When the Government didn't come to the Highlands the people were savages and very bad, lived in caves, in holes, for there is a fight between clan or clan against clan, little food were planted in small gardens but there is robbery every night. When a person grew thin because of hunger, his friends took him and burned him alive threw him in holes or buried him. When a man built himself a house surrounded by a fence and garden the other people came to rob his crops while he is in his little house and heard them he would trick them by touching something in the door and robbers taught (sic) he went out so they shot their arrows at him until the arrows were gone he went out unhurt and they stole all the food. Therefore many people died, some went to their neighbours during the night when they heard that he has food.

The explorers led by Mr. Taylor, Mr. Leahy and Brothers push up to find gold and discovered the Highlands during the 1930's.

The troubles were only brought to the kiaps. Then we have Luluais and Tutuls to take up the job.

At the present time we have our own government, the Native Local Government Council to cover all the jobs.

Education starts in the highlands (Government) late during 1952. During this time the Government built many schools.

Business starts late too but it grows rapidly and the people are earning quite a big sum of money.

The crops which brought good pay are: coffee, Passionfruit, and peanut.

The people are pleased about the work of the Agriculture Department to provide or spread these businesses.

The Department of public health has provided aid posts and medical boys and nurses for the people.

*   *   *

The arrival of the Taylor-Leahy-Spinks expedition in Chimbu in 1933 was the beginning of a wholly new phase of social change — direct contact with western people. This sudden entrance of representatives of 20th-century Australia had no precedent in tribal life. Almost everything about the newcomers was different, their bodies, color, clothing, equipment and supplies, food, language, behavior, relationships with one another and with the local people. They communicated by radio and air with a world beyond the mountains of which the Chimbu had no experience. It was their first indication of the existence of this external, white man's world.

At first, the Chimbu were awestruck by this strange band of visitors who passed up the Wahgi valley and later returned. A bold attempt to steal some of their goods was stopped by the force of arms, and the power of Australian rifles was demonstrated to Chimbus for the first time. Chimbu feelings towards the Europeans were fear mixed with desire for the white man's goods. The first visitors traded shells, beads and knives for food, and these were in great demand. The new strangers were attacked for their goods, as would be any person without local friends and relatives. It was the normal Chimbu reaction to outsiders. Fighting, theft, and killing of opponents and enemies could not be quickly eradicated. Now the people gather and attack in a show of force, knowing well that the participants are liable to jail sentences. Attacks on Europeans were so quickly and severely punished that they have rarely been made in recent years. The white man's power in this respect is quite feared. But between Chimbus, conflicts, jealousies, etc. are still often met by violence.

The other weapon of revenge is sorcery, which has been a most important one in some places. Since attempted sorcery may go undetected, having no visible effect and practiced in secrecy, its frequency cannot be measured. Sorcery diagnosis and accusation in cases of misfortune are subject to some measurement, but comparison is difficult. The anthropologist has a limited time in the field, and such matters are often concealed, since these are private affairs of local groups and all Europeans are thought to be unsympathetic to sorcery beliefs. I received most of my information about sorcery from a few informants in one Mintima subclan. I judge this to be due both to the sorcery concerns of these people at that time and to my very close relations with them. I cannot conclude that this indicates a difference in the practice or in the intensity of belief. It has certainly

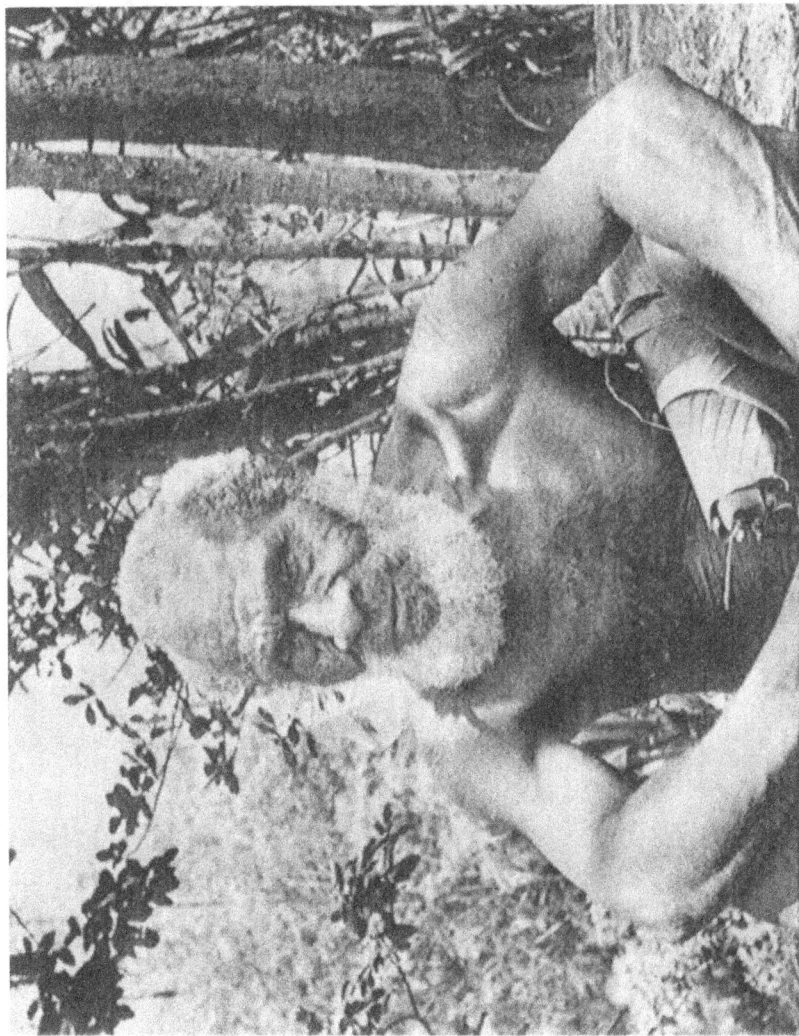

Tagumba, an ageing big man.

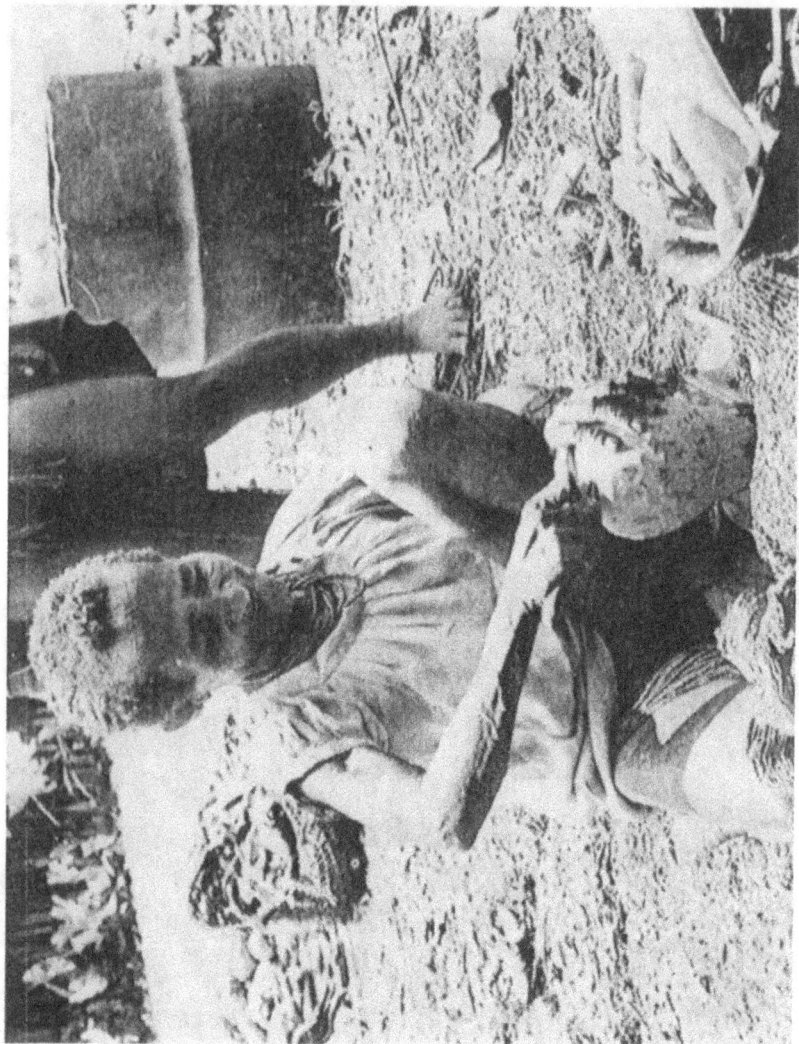

Women scrape vegetables to cook for a group. A cooking drum is ready to be filled.

A group of men clear weeds, turn over soil and dig ditches for a garden.

Sitting at a men's house, taking down a family history. Photograph by H. C. Brookfield, 1958.

The groom's group carry in the marriage payment of shells, feathers and money. It is a ceremonial occasion so men are decorated and carry spears.

Bride being taken to her husband's group. She is decorated with feathers and carries an axe, nowadays steel.

Layout of sugar cane and bananas to be distributed to funeral guests. Men are seated along the column to remind big men of the recipients designated.

A small pig feast ground: men's houses and guests' houses.

Dancers at a feast decorated with shells and feathers, carrying spears. The dance is a mock attack.

Performance at a play representing a magical rite.

Men laying out cooked vegetables and pork at a small feast. Cooking pots are now used to make rice and soup.

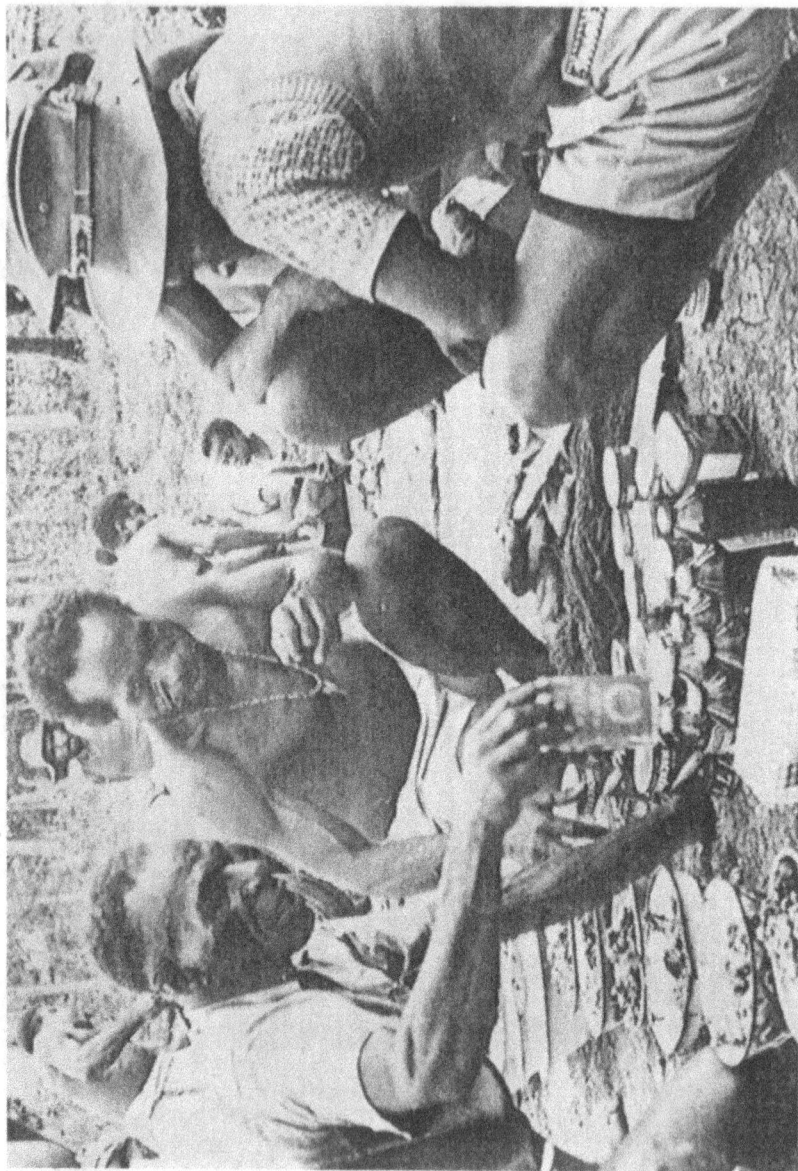

1965—an ex-tultul and two councillors putting out cooked food, beer, bread and canned foods at a modern feast.

A council meeting—Kondom President, Chimbu clerk and Australian officer at head, councillors on benches. The public was invited to observe this special outdoor session.

Kondom explaining election procedure, 1963.

Contract workers returning from plantation labor carrying drum, lamp, umbrellas, pots, suitcase and bags of goods. Photograph by H. C. Brookfield.

Girls in feather headdresses preparing to take communion at Mingende on Corpus Christi day.

been observed in other places that there are sudden outbursts of sorcery accusations, which can be clearly associated with frictions and conflicts within the group.

Over the years, the suppression of fighting and the extension of public roads has produced a significant change in Chimbu attitudes. Chimbus were, for the first time, safe in their homes from unprovoked attacks, and could travel without fear of ambush or robbery (Nilles 1953). The people gained confidence in European instruction and medicine, so that they turned to mission and government for help and guidance. They readily accepted the materials of the white man, eager to acquire clothing, steel tools, blankets, cookware, beads and other decorative objects. They want the living standards that they see the white man enjoying, his modern-style houses, and their furnishings and facilities, his cars, his airplanes, clothing, etc.

But consider what is the Chimbu view of these new things. Their participation and knowledge of the white man's world is circumscribed by their education, status and traditional thought patterns. They do not enter the mission or government station as equal members. They are regarded as primitives, ignorant, clumsy, and, to some extent at least, incapable of understanding what they see. Chimbu infancy and childhood, where basic life attitudes and knowledge are gained, are in the huts and in the fields. When I entered an unfamiliar area, the small children were very frequently carried up to me and told by their parents to feel my skin and my clothing. When we had a jeep in the area, children and adults very often came up just to look at it and feel the metal and rubber on the car. The origin and process of manufacture of these things were completely unknown to the people who behaved in this way.

The first people and the first contacts were with the government officers and the mission. The Chimbus reacted with mixtures of fear and uncertainty. In the first few years, young people were attached to government and mission posts as domestic servants and field workers, watching the ways of the white man. They did not enter into any relationships that were of a usual or familiar character, and most of the activities that they carried out were either traditional forms of labor or new skills, such as cooking, washing clothes, making beds, milking cows, etc., which they were taught while at work. Their view of the white man's world was developed from these contacts, activities and relationships. They did not see the world of industry or government. They observed only the outpost, colonial situation. All of their contacts with this outside world were mediated through their individual associations with government and mission personnel. This regulated their communication, their goods, their power, and immediately demonstrated a superior technology and knowledge of economy and processes.

The colonial situation in central New Guinea consists first, of a visit from Europeans and their New Guinean entourage. In time government and missionary posts, and perhaps traders and settlers come in. Building materials and some simple carpentry and other household machinery are brought in from outside. The natives can only suppose that these goods and machines are somehow created or made at some distant place: the process is the white man's secret. The sequence of mining, smelting of metals and processing and manufacturing of these goods is completely unknown and never demonstrated. The local people see at most the coming and going of messages and transport vehicles, the unloading of crates and parcels from ships, trucks or airplanes, and the appearance of some skilled personnel to put together these parts and then make or erect the marvelous objects of the white man.

In 1965, hand weaving on simple looms was demonstrated in preparation for introducing a cottage industry. One of the councillors said, "We thought cloth and blankets were made by the spirits. Now we can see how it is done."

Social, political and economic processes are even more mysterious than these imported objects. The collection of taxes and allocation of budgets and monies for various developmental projects, the organization of school curricula and the training of teachers, medical training, experiments, and the interpretation of diagrams, books and pharmacopoeia; indeed, the whole body of western knowledge never really reaches the Chimbus.

These lacks of knowledge about western procedures and processes lead to some quite fantastic interpretations of things. The Chimbus in my area raised rather scrawny chickens and sold them, when they could, for the equivalent of about $3.00. At the same time, it was possible to buy imported, canned chickens for about half that price. When this discrepancy was pointed out to Kondom, one of the leading men and more sophisticated than most, he commented, "Well, yes, of course, the canned chickens are made in a factory. We bought the first chicks from the mission, and we raise and feed them for a long time before they are sold."

Chapter 13

The Forces of Change

THE CHIMBU could see the forces of change in individual or personified terms. The *kiap* (in larger stations, "number one *kiap*") was the first and after that the most important representative of the Australian administration. He was the boss of the native police (*kimberi nim,* the Chimbu term for "Father of the Arrow") and interpreters (*turnimtok* in Pidgin) as well as, in time, a staff of junior officers. The *kiap* was census-taker, administrator, judge, law interpreter and director of a number of labor and other enterprises, such as road work. He appointed and supervised the *bosbois, tultuls* and *luluais* and he was the mediator between the local people and any special officers or other white men, such as traders and missionaries.

The highlands were at first outposts of New Guinea coastal districts Sepik and Morobe, with only junior officers posted to the highland stations. For about 20 years, administrative staff at Kundiawa consisted of one *kiap*. Chimbu was first a Patrol Post and later a Sub-District, with a native population of about 150,000. It is now a District, with over 180,000 people. During the 1930's, only those within three or four miles of Kundiawa were in any frequent contact with the Chimbu Post. Patrol Officers had as their first duty the institution of peace and order. They were almost continually engaged in attempting to stop fights and tribal warfare, riding horses on newly-constructed tracks to quickly reach the scene of trouble. These *kiaps* were supported by a small force of native police, usually men from an area which had been under Australian administration for some years.

Gradually they brought local Chimbu leaders under administrative influence. Many of these had been engaged in fights and disturbances, arrested, and while in *kalabus,* received instruction and encouragement so that they supported the administration's policy of suppression of tribal warfare. During this early period, there were perhaps twenty such men in the Kundiawa jail at any one time. As prisoners they were not punished, but rather instilled with administrative principles and procedures. About 300 headmen (*bosbois*) were appointed by the *kiaps.* These were men who, the officers felt, could dominate and command in disturbances in their own groups; six of them were then recommended as *luluai* when such appointments were permitted in the late 1930's, a *bosboi* was expected to bring offenders to the *kiap* without help by the police. The *kiap* endeavored to make the *bosboi* respected and obeyed, and their position depended more upon administration support than upon the authority which they naturally held as big men within their groups.

Chimbu were always on the brink of tribal warfare. In 1938, one *kiap,* K. Vial, with surveyors, prepared a map showing tribal boundaries as at the time of the beginning of Australian administration in 1933-4. It was hoped that this would regularize tribal territories and prevent further outbreaks of warfare. It did not fully succeed, for the boundary location was rarely considered just by all parties, and conflicts have continued, but this map has only been modified in some particulars by recent decisions of the Lands Commission.

The Chimbus saw at Kundiawa a succession of *kiaps* who stressed various aspects of their role as representatives of the Australian administration. Some were very enthusiastic about roads or hygiene, others about the law and order aspect of their jobs. To some, the intensification of control within a limited area was foremost, while others wished especially to extend control on the fringes of the area. A 1940 report for the Chimbu area states that tribal fighting had nearly ceased, and the headmen and *luluais* could be relied upon to bring in offenders. A census had been taken of many groups, but by no means all the people came to give their names to the officer. The conditions of peace permitted many to return to their former land, as their enemies could no longer drive them away. At this time, there were 13 miles of vehicular roads and 339 miles of bridle paths in the area patrolled from Chimbu.

In the first few years of administration, a single officer covered a large and densely populated area in an effort to stop tribal fighting, build roads and develop communications. During the war in 1942-5, the military administration, ANGAU, concentrated on establishing tribal peace and redirecting energies formerly used in fighting to road-building.

Aside from the provision of better communication, road work was regarded as a good way to utilize energies which might otherwise be devoted to fighting. It remains the chief form of public works undertaken. Much work is still done by hand, and the casuarina wood bridges required continuous replacement. Since 1960, when coffee production was widely established, minor roads have been extended into many areas where vehicles rarely go, and these roads are always in need of repair.

After the resumption of civil administration in 1946, *luluais* were generally appointed as tribal leaders and *tultuls* as heads of segments. The *tultul* was supposed to be a village leader who was familiar with European ways and able to speak Pidgin English. He should explain and interpret between the government and the people. The *luluais* and *tultuls* were expected to keep peace and bring offenders to the *kiap* for adjudication. This, then, was a system of indirect rule, following the British principle of indirect rule as applied in Africa and elsewhere. Their authority, such as it was, depended upon their position as big men in the traditional political system, and on their recognition by the *kiap* as men of leadership potential in their groups. Officers patrolled the district regularly and stopped in each area to take a census, note progress and problems, once a year at least.

The old warrior leaders were appointed as headmen responsible for preventing war, settling minor disputes, reporting disturbances, and directing public works. These men could not draw upon traditional institutions or values as the basis for their new roles; peace between tribes was never before a goal. The appointed headmen could only rely upon the administration's enforcement of law and order to maintain their control. This reliance upon the Australian officers continues to the present.

The administrative policy was to guide the people to political progress, and to extend control, peace and order through the influence of the Australian officers, police, and native-appointed officials. In the early days, the native official was a kind of unpaid local policeman (in Papua the office was called village constable) whose job was to bring offenders to the European officer for judgment and punishment. During the 1940's and 1950's, Chimbu native officials became permanent and titled, wearing "brass" — badges or other emblems of office. There were one or two *luluais* for a tribe of 1,500 to 4,000 people, and there were *tultuls* for one or two subclans with a population of 100 to 300 people. The New Guinea administration of law, under Australian rule, which began in the early 1920's, derives from the Queensland (Australia) Criminal Code adapted to local conditions.

In the early days, the *kiap* and his native police were most urgently involved in cases which led to assault or fighting, but as Australian influence spread, disputes were brought to the *kiap* by *luluais* and *tultuls*. In practice, a great many disputes were settled by the *luluais, tultuls,* or an informal group of people who combined to stop a fight from developing. Other cases were decided by the combined force of *luluais, tultuls,* police and interpreters, without ever reaching the *kiap's* attention. (See Ch. 17).

The powers of *luluais, tultuls,* police, etc. were clearly defined in Australian law, but this was never truly conveyed to the Chimbu people. What arose in Chimbu was a local understanding of these powers as influenced by the traditional rights of big men, by the fear of the *kiap,* and his interference in local disputes, with the use of police from Chimbu and other districts, and interpreters as mediators between the *kiap* and the local people. A resolution of disputes between Chimbu was, in fact, rare. *Kiap,* police, interpreter, *luluai* and *tultul* alike usually told disputants to stop quarreling, restore damages, and go back home to live peacefully. This frequently sufficed, because the disputants feared the *kiap* and the threat of jail.

There was always a thin line between the esteem of a big man and the chance that he would overstrain his followers, demand too much and lose their support. As the appointed head of a specific group, the native official's following was assigned by the Australian officer, and assigned for life. The traditional checks on the power of leaders could not be made. The appointment of *tultul* and *luluai* was a complete innovation for the Chimbu, as it defined the group of followers quite specifically in terms of census units, and it gave them the power to apply to the Australian officers for support, rather than to the following that they themselves had been able to acquire. The native official was judged as efficient or inefficient by the Australian officer observing his ability to get work done, to bring people to the station for hearing disputes, or to the officer on tour for census and other official matters. These were quite different from the traditional big men's activities. His following could fail to support him either because his authority was insufficient or because of their dislike of the administration's policies or regulations.

The first *luluais* and *tultuls* were the leaders of their day, men prominent in war and ceremony, active leaders, not always adaptable to the new ways of gaining respect and keeping order. When they died, aged, or proved incapable, they were replaced by suitable younger men. In the 1950's, some of these younger native officials had some slight familiarity with the administration and Europeans as former employees, apparently progressive young men who were expected to lead in new developments. The administration was no longer mainly devoted to preventing tribal warfare, but beginning to introduce cash crops and extend social services and education.

From 1945 onward, there were more regularized services, and the extension of influence and control throughout the area, more regular census patrols, with new patrol posts in many places hitherto unexplored, and more officers in the older posts. Medical, educational and agricultural services were established.

Until 1959, the system of appointed officials, adopted throughout New Guinea for native administration, was used in the Chimbu area. In 1959, central Chimbu was organized into the Waiye Local Government Council, bringing together four tribes, about 10,000 people. Councils can be a dramatic step towards local government. A group of former enemy tribes are joined together. Councillors are elected, and participate in regular meetings, planning community development. The council collects taxes and allocates its income. A new council is elected every two years, so it is more responsive to the will of the people than are the *luluais* and *tultuls,* who are appointed for life by the Australian officers.

When the council was established, the local groupings were revised and one councillor was often to be elected by a new group of two subclans which had formerly two or more *tultuls.* This gave each councillor a much larger population and territory than had the former *tultuls,* and usually put him in charge of a group which had not formerly been allied under any single leader, big man or government official. The problems of maintaining order and cooperation in this larger group were sometimes insurmountable.

During the 1960's, there were a number of further developments in the administrative system to specialize the diverse activities of Australian Native Affairs Officers as administrators of local government councils, cooperatives, Lands Commissioners, circuit-court judges, etc. At District and Sub-District stations there were representatives of a number of special services.

The Agricultural Officers stationed at Kundiawa were chiefly concerned with the development of cash crops, concentrating upon coffee growing and the improvement of coffee processing. They were also active in helping the local people to acquire equipment to be used in coffee processing. After 1964, when the Chimbu cooperative was established, there were close ties between agricultural and cooperative officers to further develop the coffee industry.

The Medical Officer worked mainly in Kundiawa, where the largest number and most serious cases came and some surgery could be performed. Doctors and Medical Assistants stationed at Kundiawa and other posts sometimes went on health, nutrition and hygiene patrols to give injections or conduct malaria, yaws, tuberculosis, etc. surveys. In the Infant Welfare Service, nurses visit outlying areas to examine the babies, give some treatment and take the seriously ill into the hospital for treatment. There were also, throughout the area, Medical Aid Posts staffed by a native trained Medical Orderly, which were way-stations to which sick people could go for treatment of minor injuries, illnesses and malaria. These orderlies also sent word for their seriously-ill patients to be picked up and taken to the hospital as required.

A small school was established in Kundiawa before the Second World War, but it closed during the war. Another school was established in 1947, but little government education was provided for many years. After 1960, the government began a "crash program" of new schools, intensifying elementary education, using teachers who had been through a brief training course. In these schools are both Australian and New Guinean trained teachers, mostly teaching the first two or three grades of the curriculum, which is a special adaptation of the Australian educational system for the territory. Those students who successfully complete the first few grades as taught in their local schools can sometimes gain admission to a higher grade in Kundiawa, and some of these later reach a more advanced school, or the Kerowagi High School. During the 1960's, a very few Chimbu boys acquired sufficient education to become native clerks and other trainees for specialized, literate, and skilled occupations. There is a technical school at Kundiawa, which is where boys learn simple skills of carpentry and handling of tools and machinery. Other social services included the occasional organization of women's club activities, in which women were given some instruction in baby care, hygiene, cooking, sewing and sports. Some other adult education was also planned.

Both Catholic and Lutheran missions began in the Chimbu area in 1934, and they have grown through the years to set up new stations and schools. Both the Catholic priests and Lutheran ministers often spend many years at the same place, learn the local language, and form close ties with individuals and families. I attended the funeral ceremonies for Father Schaefer in 1958. Many thousands of Chimbus came to pay their respects at that mass, and many of them described his role: he came to their homes, visiting the old and the sick, when they needed him most. He spoke their language and understood them.

The Catholic mission at Mingende had the greatest influence among the Naregu people with whom I worked. It is near the boundary area between Naregu, Siambuga-Wauga and Nauru tribal groups, which for many years would not participate in joint feasts for fear of "poison" or sorcery. Mingende is a large church, with regular and well-attended services. On the important festival occasions of Christmas, Easter and Corpus Christi, Mingende is attended by thousands of people, who take part in outdoor services, parades, plays, entertainments and sports.

At Mingende and throughout the region, there are schools for adults being prepared for conversion and baptism, and elementary schools for children, which teach elementary literacy, numbers, and general knowledge. Those mission schools taught by trained native and European lay teachers, nuns and priests reach a more advanced standard than the small community schools, and are subsidized by the administration.

Aside from religious practice and education, the priest's main interest seems to center on family life. He baptizes the children of converts, performs marriage services, usually some time after the native marriage ceremonies, and advises on marital and family problems. Thus members of the church may be torn between using the priest's counsel and the government's courts to decide serious issues when marriage ends in separation and divorce is contemplated. The church requires that its converts be monogamous, and a man with several wives has to give up all but one of them if he is to be converted. This is a serious issue, since the most prominent big men in traditional Chimbu affairs have a number of wives, and can indeed only maintain their position by the combined efforts of many wives in providing food, pigs, etc. for their large contributions to ceremonial affairs. The polygamous big man cannot become a convert without losing the economic support for his position, and the decision may be difficult. The church also has a shop in which clothing, food, tools and some other imported goods are sold. The hospital, staffed by nuns and assistants, is mainly used by women in childbirth. The Catholic mission has selected from traditional practice: it encourages natives to wear their traditional decorations on festive church occasions and prohibits ritual practices connected with ancestors which seem to conflict with Catholic teaching. The mission's farm has cattle and horses, and has introduced some new strains of pigs and chickens.

The Lutherans have long been established in Kundiawa (Ega) and Kerowagi with churches, schools, farms and shops. On the whole, the Lutherans permit their converts less participation in traditional practices than do the Catholics: at the pig feast, Lutheran converts had a cluster of houses on the edge of the ceremonial area when the tribe gave its ceremony and were only permitted to participate in the killing and distribution of pigs.

The Catholics support the substitution of Catholic for Chimbu rites at feasts and ceremonies, and place a cross at the ceremonial center (*bolum*) in the pig feast. Often the priest blesses the ceremony and the pigs before they are killed. The missionaries preach against sorcery, witchcraft, magic, spirits, etc., so that these beliefs and practices are suppressed. This does not eliminate beliefs, but people are unwilling to talk about them or practice openly. Since many ritual, magical and sorcery practices have always been private or secret, they have been even more concealed in recent years.

But Chimbu continue to fear sorcery; at times of epidemic illness and sudden death there is talk of expelling suspected sorcerers.

Another force for change in the area is the European traders and settlers. In fact, there are very few of these within the Chimbu area, since the land is so limited that the government has not permitted leasing of large tracts to outsiders; but there are some shops run by Australians and by New Guineans from other areas. A large privately-owned coffee purchasing and shipping establishment near Kundiawa later became the Chimbu cooperative, and wholly native-owned in 1964. Many Chimbu work as casual laborers on coffee plantations in the Eastern and Western Highlands Districts. There are also many men engaged in domestic household cleaning, cooking and laundry work for Europeans in the area. This kind of work is really on-the-job training. The chief domestic employee of a household is known as the *mankimasta,* and he is in charge of the smaller boys (*mankis*) who are learning to do domestic work. At Kundiawa and other centers Chimbus — both local and employed — become acquainted with New Guineans from other Districts who work at a range of clerical, technical, skilled and unskilled jobs. These contacts are an important influence for change.

Finally, there has been "agreement labor" from 1950 onwards: Chimbus are recruited to work on coastal plantations for a two-year period. Many of them have long been employed as carriers or other unskilled laborers. While on the coastal plantations they live in barrack-like buildings but have some opportunity to visit new places and towns in the coastal areas. One acquisition is knowledge of lucky, a gambling game. At the end of their contract they return home with goods and cash. The goods are frequently distributed among leading older men of their group. Often, this is the first stage in the accumulation of a marriage payment to be made on behalf of the young returned worker. By the middle 1960's, nearly every young man had experienced some period of work away from home. Married men also, fairly often, went away to work. In some areas, the absence of men had a serious effect upon family life, agricultural productivity, health and welfare, but for the most part the effect on any one family was limited. The labor gives men experience in the white man's ways that women do not share. They almost always become fluent in Pidgin and habituated to new forms of work, food, shelter and clothing. Only after the women's club became organized, about 1964, would women speak and indicate that they understood Pidgin; but all of the young men that I had known could speak fluent Pidgin from 1958 or earlier.

These then, are the varied forces of change which have influenced the local people in the Chimbu area. Primarily, this was through the administration, with the Native Affairs officers and a wide range of educational,

medical, agricultural and social welfare officers. While the individual officers are frequently changed, the government and its many native assistants
from other parts of the territory, working as police and various training
officers, has an impact, not only in the Kundiawa headquarters, but
throughout the region. The police, technical assistants, clerks and other
Papuan and New Guinean headquarters personnel have more personal
relations with local Chimbus than do the Europeans. They form an inter-
mediate class, both respected and resented by the local Chimbus.

Traders, visitors and plantation owners have less influence, except occasionally as long-resident individuals within a limited area. The impressions
of European settlers, Papuans and New Guineans in other parts of the
territory which are brought back to Chimbu by their young people who
have traveled and worked with them are probably among the greatest
forces towards change and also towards unity of the territory as a whole.
The past 20 years has brought an entirely new class of Chimbu: the
permanently employed, who visit their home groups only for short periods
of leave or between jobs, and do not maintain any fields or houses on
home land.

Chapter 14

Material and Technological Change

TRADITIONALLY, anthropologists and archaeologists have often studied the material culture of a people. These are the most immediately observable aspects of culture, most readily studied outside the context of social communication. Archaeological remains and their dating, the material equipment of a people before any contact with the western world, and the substitution of imported objects for native manufactures, are all observable and measurable features. The elements of material culture can be counted and classified.

We have a good deal of information concerning the changes and trends in change of material culture and technology in Chimbu, since discovery in 1934. Reports and observations have been written by government officers, missionaries, and other observers over the years. My own notes from 1958 onwards provide more detailed data for the area in which I worked. Even had the Chimbu not been as interested in material goods and the new things of the white man as they are, the changes in material culture still would be better documented than the more elusive changes in religious belief and political activities.

The most immediately evident differences among peoples are their physical characteristics, clothing and material goods. No language or comprehension of meaning need accompany the evidence of vision, smell and touch. The impression made by the Taylor, Leahy and Spinks expedition to the highlands is still a source of story and awe. At first, they could not distinguish between the white man's skin, his clothing and his shoes. Perhaps — and we have a considerable number of suggestions concerning this, although I am absolutely convinced of none — they thought the white men and their New Guinean entourage were spirits from another world, or ancestors. Such belief fits in very well with what we consider to be "cargo" thinking: the belief that the ancestors are sending to the people the wonderful goods and manufactures of the western world, and these are being blocked in delivery by interfering white men at the docks. (Cf. Burridge 1960; Strathern 1971.) If the departed local people have indeed become godlike creators of western plenty, and wish to give them to their descendants, then the fact that these western goods are now controlled by white men must surely indicate some interference by the white men of today. But this kind of assumption of a belief system has too often been made and too often applied to all Melanesians. The facts for Chimbu are not nearly so well substantiated.

However, whether or not the first white men to come to the Chimbu area were believed to be spirits, it remains unquestioned that they were regarded as the possessors of the most marvelous goods ever seen by Chimbu. The first visitors offered shells, metal axes and knives for food. The large gold-lip and green snail shells of coastal New Guinea that they had for trade were much larger and more valuable than the broken fragments of shells which had hitherto been used in native ornament and exchange.

Mick Leahy recounts his first visit to the Chimbu in which he noticed the oblong houses on ridge tops, the ditches and garden squares, the fences, terraces, spears, axes, shields, bird-of-paradise feathers and small shells. Some of these characteristics distinguished Chimbu from neighboring peoples with a different style of architecture, garden preparation and set of equipment. The bird-of-paradise, parrot and hawk feathers and plumes, and the shells, were for the most part imported into the Chimbu region, but once in Chimbu, marriage and other transactions carried them from person to person and group to group. Axe blades and axes were exchanged throughout the highlands. The Chimbu certainly were familiar with valuable objects which were not produced in their immediate environment.

Leahy also says: "The people of this village showed us a few steel scraping and gouging tools that they had, mere fragments of old knife blades, the size of one's finger nail, fastened to bits of wood. These tools, poor as they were, must have been infinitely superior to stone for such purposes as shaping arrowheads. By local standards, the steel tools in our packs were doubtless more valuable than the gold we had come to seek." (Leahy and Crain 1937: 158.)

The interest that the Chimbu had in the expedition is shown. "Natives in hundreds swarmed about our camp as soon as the tents were up, the men and our assistants parking their spears by sticking them in the ground about a hundred yards away. The cluster of spears soon gave the appear-

ance of a thicket. We all decided, after a look at this crowd, that they con-
stituted the finest looking group of natives we had ever seen in New
Guinea." (*Ibid.* 160.) A little further to the west, the following incident
took place: "A force of spearmen quickly gathered and advanced toward
us, shouting defiance, spreading out across our path behind their shields
decorated with cassowary plumes. . . . Taylor's confident bearing and
diplomacy won them over, however, and presently he waved for the column
to proceed. After some hesitation, the new natives marched ahead with us
to a camping place where a number of old garden beds were lying fallow.
When we brought out the shell trade, there was a rush to bring us pigs and
kai-kai [food] and a fine-looking warrior, who acted as spokesman for
the people, made signs to indicate that we were welcome to remain there
for further trade." (*Ibid.* 162, 163.) It was at this point in the Wahgi
valley that a landing-strip was built, and a small native police force was
left to guard it. They were later attacked by natives who wanted to take
over the trade goods of the white man. When a plane landed on the
quickly-prepared landing field in the Wahgi valley, the natives apparently
believed that the plane was an animal. When out of the plane came, not
just white men, but also stores of goods for trade, the natives brought up
food and pigs and other trading material to begin trading with the monster
animal which came bearing white man's goods.

It was evident to all, as he settled into the area and began his administrative, exploratory, missionary, prospecting, and other activities, that the
white man was much better off than the Chimbu. He did not work, and
the goods came to him from the sky or were carried in by a line of native
carriers. Some of these goods were consumed by the white man; others
were used for trade to get food and labor. The food came readily prepared
in packages and cans. There was no land clearing, planting, harvesting and
cleaning that could be observed by the Chimbus. The goods which the
white man brought with him were strong and powerful. His blankets were
warm, his clothes were sturdy, his shoes were strong, his tools were powerful
and efficient, and the whole collection of metal, leather, cloth, etc., goods
were very useful and reliable objects. Beads and bangles were classified
with shells and other objects which had always been considered ornaments and valuables to Chimbu. The distinction between the naturally
produced shell and the manufactured plastic or glass ornament could
hardly be made by a Chimbu, who had seen neither ocean nor factory.

There were some even greater wonders. Matches are far superior to the
time-consuming, friction-produced fires of the old days. Lamps and fuel
were entirely new; in 1958, whenever I lit my pressure-lamp, a large
crowd gathered to watch and gasp at the wonderful moment when it
flared up and became a bright light. They were no better able than I to

comprehend why the fire sometimes failed or the mantle disintegrated.

It is little wonder that these goods and equipment of the white man were associated with magic and other extraordinary circumstances. This was most evident to me in my first year, 1958, in Chimbu, while later I think greater familiarity with me and knowledge about the white man dispersed some of these fantastic beliefs. But during my early field trips, the Chimbus very frequently stole and collected my discarded metal, paper, plastic, etc., household objects as white man's treasures. For example, our first field trip was equipped with, as it turned out, two defective kerosene Primus stoves. We put parts of them together and made one that would work. The remaining parts, which had unrepairable defects, were taken by our assistant to his own house. He said that he was making a collection of the white man's things. He also had, and carried about with him most of the time, a tin biscuit box which had been given to him by an employer many years earlier, and in the box, as I remember, a broken comb and a toothbrush. When he had matches, cigarettes, and other such things, he also kept them in this box. One day, he came to me in great tears of distress because the toothbrush had broken. At that time, the people of that area had very little money, and no nearby shops to supply such ordinary household objects as these.

At the end of my first field trip, I prepared to give away a collection of worn clothing and household equipment. When this became generally known, the result was a rather violent mob, pushing and grabbing at these things. My storage shed was several times broken into, in the early days, but after they had some cash income and purchased their own goods, my household discards were ignored, and theft was rare. Later, they did ask for items which we had that were not to be found in local shops, such as particular types of hats or other clothing, and a heavy tarpaulin. Ornamental objects were always appealing to the Chimbu, and fitted rapidly into their miscellaneous collection of headgear, belts, necklaces, armbands, etc. In the cold night climate of Chimbu, warm things, and particularly blankets, were highly valued. Often towels were worn around the shoulders as a shawl. The immediate desires of Chimbu for white man's goods, then, were compounded of interest in novelties and appreciation of the strength or efficiency of this equipment.

We have an excellent account from Father John Nilles, describing his observations of the Chimbu people from 1937 to the early 1950's. In the paper published in 1953, he remarks that the digging stick is to a large extent now replaced by iron spades, shovels and pickaxes. Wooden hoes and spades were hardly ever seen. Bush knives and axes of steel were taking the place of native bamboo knives and stone axes. Razor blades were used for cutting hair, shaving and carving. Sewing needles were replacing the bone awl, safety pins, nails and pieces of scrap iron were widely used. Many new food plants were introduced and widely grown, either for consumption or sale to the Europeans. European pigs, fowl, and dogs were replacing or breeding with native varieties; cats and goats were less common. Enamel pots, billy-cans, tin drums, were used for cooking; plates, dishes, cups, bottles, forks, spoons, were all being used. The native manufacture of salt was quickly supplanted by imported European salt. Native tobacco was quickly replaced by new varieties, and smoking was with pipes, strips of newspaper as cigarette paper, or, as I saw later on, store purchases of cigarette papers, tobacco and cigarettes.

Houses of native materials, but built above ground on piles, with floors, higher walls and grass-thatched roofs, became known as "mission" houses. In the early 1950's, some of these were fitted with plank doors on hinges, hasps, locks and nails. Many people kept their especially valued possessions in locking suitcases or boxes. Very few natives wore European garments in 1950, and most of these were workers on mission and government stations.

On my first visit to the Chimbu area in 1958, money and European goods were used to a small extent in a number of different ways. Some of the men, but hardly any of the women and children, wore European clothing in the form of *laplap* (wrap-around cloths), shorts, shirts, and sweaters. Rucksacks, boxes and suitcases were highly valued but rare. Every family had at least one steel axe and most of them also had one or more knives and shovels. There were a few other tools such as small saws, hammers, etc. in general use. Most houses were built entirely of native materials — nails, hinges, and padlocks were very rare. A few families had some cutlery, metal or enamel cooking pots, and dishes. Most cooking was done in the traditional earth ovens or over embers.

In 1958 the Chimbu were only beginning to use money. Their subsistence technology was only slightly modified by the introduction of a few items of European manufacture, some clothing, tools and housewares. The little money they had was mostly used in marriage and death payments and in gambling. After 1959, taxes were assessed by the Waiye Local Government Council, beginning at ten shillings (U.S. $1.12) for an adult man and two shillings for a woman, and rising to £2 (U.S. $4.50) for men and ten shillings for women in 1965. In the first years, income was so small that many were unable to pay this tax, but its requirement forced everyone to sell some produce or labor for cash. In speeches and discussions, tax was an important element in the drive for Chimbu economic progress. All local government councillors were economically ambitious and encouraged everyone to work, sell produce and increase his income. Modern-style houses were built for councillors by their constituents, to serve as a model for all.

The largest store in Kundiawa, part of a chain of European trader-owned shops in New Guinea, displayed the following miscellany for sale in 1963:

Clothing: shirts, blouses, dresses, cut and seamed lengths of cloth for *laplaps,* bolts of cloth, belts, hats, shoes, sandals.

Household: large basins, cooking pots, mugs, drinking glasses, teapots, plates, frying pans, percolators, flashlights, batteries, kerosene pressure lamps, hurricane lamps, cushions, canvas for cots, buckets, suitcases, padlocks, money boxes, key chains, transistor radios, bags, kerosene, matches, mats, blankets, towels, sewing-machine oil, glass louvers, spades, knives, hinges, ripsaws, hammers, axes, bush saws, bush knives.

Food: tinned fish, tinned meat, tinned chicken, powdered coffee, flour, biscuits, cheese, fruit drink, sugar, tea.

Other goods: swimming goggles, toys, Japanese fans, umbrellas, marbles, playing cards, peroxide, note paper and envelopes, razor blades, shaving soap, brilliantine, talcum powder, cigarettes, chewing gum, bracelets, beads, footballs, guitars, soap and cleaners, mirrors, dye.

In 1958 there were no Chimbu-owned shops in Naregu. By 1963 there were three, but they were rarely open and had few goods for sale. They often were unable to procure supplies from Kundiawa or to obtain delivery. Supplies to local shops were unreliable and common items such as kerosene and sugar were often unavailable. In 1964-65, there were ten small shops licensed in the Naregu area to serve a population of 2,500. There was a bakery in 1967. Shop buildings were put up near the principal operator's men's house close to a path or road. Stocks and prices varied considerably — one local shop charged twice as much for rice and three-quarters as much for meat as another. In 1970, H. C. Brookfield noted twenty-six trade stores in the same area.

List of items sold in a Naregu native-owned shop in 1965:

Clothing: *laplaps,* blouses, shirts, shorts, tee-shirts.

Household: nails.

Food: rice, sugar, salt, tinned fish, tinned meat and cereal, biscuits, bread, corned beef, cooking fat.

Other goods: soap, tobacco, cigarettes, paper, beads, razor blades, chewing gum, talcum powder.

Another Naregu shop had for sale:

Laplaps, shirts, rice, tinned fish, biscuits, cigarettes, tobacco, soap, razors and blades, towels.

Perhaps the most obvious change in material goods since 1958 was in clothing. I saw bark cloth manufactured in 1958, and it was given to brides in the early 1960's but has dropped from use. Women made most of the

Chimbu clothing which consisted of fiber twine and netted goods. Now net caps, twine skirts and net aprons are little worn — only the net carrying-bags are still in general use. In 1958, mission trade stores sold old, discarded and inappropriate clothing to grateful Chimbus. Old serge vests, American school sweat shirts, puffed-sleeved blouses and rubber hats were worn by men, and torn strips of cloth were used for loincloths and women's skirts. Towels and torn blankets were worn around the head or shoulders. Most people had a belt or beads of foreign manufacture. In 1965, most men, women and children had new cotton clothing. The women's club bought sewing machines with contributions and many women learned simple sewing. Men who had worked for Europeans as domestic servants could wash, iron and sew seams and buttons. Older men and women were sometimes dressed in traditional garments with cotton shirts, belts, etc. added. Old scraps of cloth, worn and inappropriate clothing were hardly ever seen. However, in 1971 the Naregu were preparing for a pig feast and performing plays for visiting tourist buses. I saw more beards, traditional net clothing, woven belts and arm bands, feathers and shells than in the early 1960's — the ceremonial activity apparently has stimulated the wearing of traditional clothes and finery.

New foods and some old foods were often boiled in pots or pan fried and eaten from plates with cutlery. Every Chimbu household had a supply of pots and pans, enamel dishes, mugs, basins and metal cutlery. These were taken to feasts and used for the family's share of the cooked food.

Most families had a wide range of European tools, including axes, shovels, hammers, saws and several kinds of knives. By 1965 a few men built more permanent houses with some purchased materials; nails, hinges, and padlocks were common, but houses with a corrugated-iron roof, windows, plank walls, and/or concrete floor were exceptional. New building styles with raised floors resulted in unheated houses, and blankets were a new necessity. Clothes and valuables were kept in suitcases and rucksacks. Some wire and barbed-wire fencing was used, especially after 1963 when some cattle were purchased and fenced in. If a man wanted unusual building and fencing materials, he had to find ways to get them from town stores through friends or local shop-keepers.

There was no simple, inevitable train of development. For example, when there was a little bit of cloth available and some wool yarn, it was picked apart and intermingled with the local plant fibers in making twine skirts, net aprons, bags and caps. Somewhat later, the traditional net and twine garments were discarded and the manufactured shirts, blouses, shorts, skirts, etc. were used. Even later than that, after the women's club established sewing lessons, there were some sewing machines, purchased by the Club, and a few women began to buy lengths of cloth and make clothes for themselves and their children. Chimbus were accustomed to buying bread at stores in Kundiawa, but only later was there a bakery within the Chimbu area. Perhaps Chimbu housewives have now learned to bake their own bread. In this way, the wonders of western technology are first experienced with no understanding of their origin or manufacturing processes; when only fragments of steel or cloth are available, these are integrated into traditional forms. Then, when more is available, it is used as manufactured. A later stage seems to be the understanding and production of western objects themselves.

The new material culture and technology is an integration of western manufactured objects as tools, as designs, and as equipment in contemporary life. Material equipment, at any time, is a composite in which the users rarely know the origins of all the elements in their tool kit. The process of piecemeal substitution and the knowledge of alternative forms can rarely be clearly described by an observer or by the people themselves. This composite mixture is not peculiar to the material culture, but is also present in contemporary social life, other activities, religious beliefs, magical practices and ceremonial activities. For example over the years there have been a series of substitutions and variations in proportions as between feathers, shells, stone axes, steel axes, knives and money in marriage payments. The pre-European marriage payment included a number of objects such as dog-tooth necklaces, stone axes and small shells which are no longer given. If marriage payments continue as a standard practice, these objects and the recently-adopted ones, such as steel axes and large shells, may be entirely supplanted by cash payments, as has happened in many other parts of the territory. But there would be very few instances in which money or manufactured goods or western-origin objects completely supplant traditional forms, just as to us, the completely plastic house would be a manufacturer's showpiece, rather than a home.

Chapter 15

Economic Change

APART FROM the technological equipment which of course is always involved in social and economic activities, the economic system itself has been constantly varied, with some distinct trends toward monetization, a market economy, and the introduction of new economic activities: migration and labor for wages, production of crops for sale, establishment of local enterprise, and consequent changes in the allocation of resources, division of labor, and development of stratification.

The pre-European Chimbu economy was subsistence and exchange: domestic produce, labor, locally unevenly distributed resources and produce, valuables from near and distant places, and some individual travel for trade. Subsistence needs were mostly satisfied by home production, and by cooperation and sharing of labor and produce in the local group. Produce was pooled for display and prestation, competitive feasts and exchanges. The exchange relations between Chimbu include feasts, delayed reciprocal payments, sporadic mutual assistance, and rarely, barter.

Most relations between men were in a kinship idiom: father-son, brothers, surrogate parents. Most men were partly dependent upon a big man for subsistence and help in establishing a family and home. Followers contribute to the activities and feasts of their leader. The unmarried men live on his land, sleep in his house and receive food from his household. Some were relatives of the big man or of one of his wives. These dependents never had a fully independent household, but always were attached to the big man in his enterprises. When, in more recent years, big men have taken employees, 'workboys,' from outside the clan and tribe into their enterprises to help with economic activities and especially with cash-crop production, such workboys have become attached household members, much the same as the former dependents were. However, they are nowadays paid wages, or at least promised them.

Wage labor away from home is common nowadays. The Highland Labor Scheme began in 1951 to secure cheap regular labor on coastal plantations. Over the years, nearly all of the young men in the Chimbu area have volunteered for a two-year term of contract work, mostly on plantations in the coastal areas. They are taken down to the coast in groups, work on copra, cocoa, rubber, or other similar plantations as cargo boys, clearing or cutting bush, tapping rubber, carrying, planting, opening coconuts and drying coconuts. There is little training or development of skill. They live and work together, and on their time off may visit a nearby town. Most of their wages are held for the completion of their contract and only some pocket money is given them during their period of employment. Until recently, nearly all of these laborers were housed in barracks and given standardized rations of food, clothing, and other domestic items by their employers. When they finish their term of work, they are transported back to their home community, nearly always laden with blankets, metalware, and other goods which they have purchased from their final pay. Some of them make more than their wages in gambling, but then of course there are others who lose heavily. While this may seem to be the dreariest life imaginable, highlanders have for over twenty years volunteered for this work, and many have had two or three terms. The experience of seeing new places, towns, peoples and the "saltwater" is an undoubted attraction — rather like military service for American country boys.

There is also employment on European-owned coffee plantations in the highlands on a daily or monthly basis. Here, working conditions are much less restrictive than on contract labor, and they come and go, visit and are visited by their friends and families from home quite frequently. Besides plantation labor, a good many Chimbu work as domestic servants for Europeans, and are to be found nearly all over the territory as cooks, laundryboys, and houseboys. Some are also attached to the government station or to missions as domestic, garden or farm employees. Those entering any sort of technical or professional service — carpenters, truck drivers, shopkeepers, military forces, policemen, agricultural extension workers, medical assistants, teachers, and clerks are fewer. Very few Chimbu have had, until very recently, the educational or technical qualifications for these jobs, and they are well aware that their education and technical training are inferior to that of many coastal peoples. This is a point of concern in the group prestige.

Now some Chimbu are permanently away in government service, plantation or domestic labor, and have their families and main social ties at their place of employment. On their occasional visits home, they are treated as distinguished guests, carrying bicycles or radios as proof of their wealth. Such Chimbu have prestige but are not very influential members of their home communities. A multi-ethnic trained labor force is developing in Papua New Guinea, especially at government and commercial centers, which is largely separate from both the surrounding peoples and from the relatives who stay at home.

In the first relations with Europeans, vegetables and pigs were exchanged for European imported and manufactured goods. This was an immediate trade, involving goods not normally exchanged against one another. (See Salisbury 1962, for a discussion of different nexuses of goods in Siane, a nearby people of the New Guinea highlands.) This established a new type of relationship, and must have convinced the Chimbu that the white man had an inexhaustible supply of these wonderful manufactured goods, since he would trade them for such common things as sweet potatoes. From that time on, Chimbu sold some food, produce and firewood to Europeans. They planted many new crops, both for home consumption and for sale, and began to distinguish their production in a new way. Formerly, there was some distinction between everyday food, primarily sweet potatoes, with some varied fruits and vegetables, and food grown mainly for feasts and entertaining, especially bananas, sugarcane and pandanus. Pigs forage and are fed sweet potatoes, especially those from the old fields, the small and scrap pieces of potato. Today, the Chimbus also grow some recently introduced vegetables, fruits and nuts (*e.g.,* tomatoes, pineapple, peanuts) primarily for sale, and many which may be either sold or consumed at home. Coffee, introduced in 1955, is wholly a cash crop. Thus, the present sale of garden produce cuts right across the former distinctions between everyday foods, feast foods and prestation items. The money which enters the system through these sources may be used for a wide range of things.

There has been some change in the amount and kinds of European goods received in exchange for food. In the direct barter of the first white travelers and settlers, trinkets and salt were exchanged against small quantities of food, metal tools and shells for large quantities of food and pigs. Standard prices were established by the government post when large-scale purchases were made for hospitals and prisons. In 1958 I paid a few shillings for a whole bunch of bananas, and bought small quantities of food for spoonfuls of salt. But, once money was established as a means of exchange, it permeated every aspect of social and economic life. Chimbu income is used for consumption, for the improvement of living standards with new and modern equipment, for investment in new and capital-producing goods, and for prestation. There are now some men with houses which use purchased materials, such as corrugated iron and timber. Contemporary big men are entrepreneurs: truck owners, coffee-pulping machine owners, men with large coffee plantations, as well as councillors, members of the board of the cooperative, and leaders of ceremonies. They are relatively large-scale consumers and owners of goods. In New Guinea, "conspicuous investment" (Finney 1969) has often been observed: a big man gets investment capital from followers, and manages the business, often assisted by a young man with some schooling. His followers continue to help him by acting as carriers or shop assistants, and the enterprise is mostly patronized by members of the shop owner's clan.

The local shops wax and wane in the fluctuating local interests and income. One shop's records showed $ A 302.49 in 1966, $ A 487.40 in 1967, $ A 593.61 in 1968.[1] Then the owner bought a car and carried goods and passengers in 1969, with a great decline in shop business. After the car deteriorated and the owner could not pay repair bills, he returned to the store, and its activity began to pick up.

The first Chimbu coffee was planted by some forward-looking leading men in the early 1950's. In about 1956 Australian Agricultural Officers supervised the laying out and planting of blocks of coffee land which were later allocated to individuals, each man having one or two rows of coffee trees. Later, men established their own coffee gardens on whatever land they had available and thought suitable. Coffee trees are a highly valued investment guarded against trespass and the loss of land in litigation. Trees of deceased men are taken over by others or reserved for their children, and the inheritance of coffee trees by orphaned boys and adopted youths is a serious matter to Chimbu. In 1958, there were 7.9 hectares of coffee planted in the Mintima area of central Chimbu (about 1,000 people). In 1967, 65.8 hectares were planted in coffee (Brookfield 1968). However, cash earnings have not increased proportionately with the amount of coffee grown. Coffee is the most important cash crop of the New Guinea highlands and few other economic opportunities exist within the region. But interest is not constant. The amount of coffee picked, processed and sold has fluctuated considerably during the period studied. This is correlated with variation in coffee prices and with the processing equipment available. Until about 1961 there was so little coffee and such desire for cash that nearly all of the coffee which became ripe was processed and carried some miles to sell in Kundiawa. But as coffee acreage increased, and older trees produced heavier crops, much was left unharvested. Some trees were planted in unsuitable soils, others were overgrown and neglected. With the growing number of coffee-bearing trees, when coffee production is at its sea-

[1] Data provided by H. C. Brookfield. All amounts are in Australian currency.

sonal peak, hand methods are inadequate to process the coffee.

Until 1964 Chimbu coffee was sold to European traders and missionaries at their stations or at road-purchasing points perhaps a mile from the grower's home. Native-grown and processed coffee is often of poor quality; it contains beans of uneven size, unripe and overripe, and one or more of the processing steps — fermenting, washing and drying — may be badly done. Thus native-grown coffee usually commands a lower price than plantation-grown coffee. Chimbus were dissatisfied about that, and in the early 1960's when the world coffee price dropped, they tried to find buyers who might offer higher prices for coffee. They also sent delegations to the government at Port Moresby to protest, as they were convinced that the European buyers in the highlands were deceiving them. But no amount of explanation could make them understand the fluctuations in world coffee prices, which resulted in variation in payments to New Guinea highlands' growers from 10¢ to 26¢ a pound for partly-dried coffee in "parchment."

Pulping to remove the soft "cherry" which surrounds the "bean" is the most time-consuming hand job of coffee processing. In the 1960's groups of Chimbus purchased pulping machines with combined contributions. The machines facilitate the work of removing the cherry to obtain the beans, but it is then necessary to ferment the beans in a vat for a day or so, and then to wash and dry them. A large picking produces a great quantity for this processing.[2] To dry, the coffee beans are spread out on a mat or blanket in front of the men's houses every day for several weeks. Someone must stay nearby to put it inside if there is a sudden rainstorm. Since women are occupied during these hours of the day when the sun is highest, in gardening and in bringing in vegetable food for the family, this work usually is done by men. But there are other uses for the time and energy of men. Thus this phase of coffee production may be neglected because of the demands of other activities. Wives normally participate with their husbands in a family coffee enterprise, working especially at weeding and picking. Only a few women are independently involved in coffee activities and these are mainly widows and the several wives of prominent men.

Several local government councillors saw European-owned coffee processing plants and demanded to have one. In 1965, with assistance from the cooperative, the Agricultural Officer and the Local Government Council, one group established a communal coffee pulping, fermenting, washing and drying plant, and later several other groups built similar ones. I saw the early operation of this first plant. About every ten days, new coffee was taken in. Each grower, often with his wife and other helpers, brought

---

[2] This coffee processing is quite different from that practiced in the French Pacific islands where the fruits fall and pulp rots before the beans are gathered. See Hanson 1970:55 ff.

his picked coffee cherries (varying from 12 to 140 pounds) to the group's plant, where it was weighed and the amount recorded. It was then pulped, fermented in concrete vats, washed in running water and dried on raised platforms along with the coffee beans of others. High quality coffee bean was produced and the best price was paid by the Cooperative. In April 1965, for about three months' accumulation of beans, men in this enterprise received from £1 (U.S. $2.25) to £17 (U.S. $38.25), varying with the quantity brought. This new group enterprise did not totally replace individual work. Many men had not subscribed the required £10 to the Cooperative, and some continued to process their own coffee and to sell to traders rather than to the Cooperative. Few men understood the procedures of share payments in the Cooperative, and even fewer the distribution in this group enterprise.

TABLE II   Composition of Marriage Payments in Central Chimbu, 1958-65

Shells:	20 goldlip mother-of-pearl shells (increased to 30 later).
	3 bailer shells.
	15 headbands decorated with cowrie shells (given until about 1960, then omitted).
Feathers:	15 pairs red bird-of-paradise feathers (*Paradisaea apoda salvadorii*).
	3 pairs yellow bird-of-paradise feathers (*P. minor finschi*).
	10 pairs black plumes (*Astrapia stephaniae*).
	1 superb bird-of-paradise feather (*Lophorina superba femina*).
	12 Pesquetts parrot (*Psittrichus fulgidus*) headdresses.
	10 other feathered headdresses, including hawk. Occasionally other plumes.
Metal goods:	20 steel axes.
	2 knives (rare in later years).
Pigs:	6 (often one or two given live).
Money:	Australian pound notes and rolls of 100 shillings, increasing from £15 in 1958 to £200 in 1965 and later.

The site of the central pulper, fermentaries, washing run, and drying racks was soon a focal point of new men's houses, storage sheds and shops. It became a central gathering place for the men of the groups concerned during the most active part of the procedure, and a showplace for all Chimbu. However, my observation of this work was limited to the first few months of its operation and I understand that subsequently many men have returned to a more individual kind of coffee processing activity, and sell to private traders. The irregular coffee collection and dispersion of payments, fluctuation of prices, and publicity of dispersion, did not suit those who wanted money for their own interests and transactional relationships. Epstein (1968: 114-33) discusses Tolai cocoa sales, which are often given to private traders for less money than to the Cocoa Project with payment delayed. In 1971, none of these group processing activities were in operation. Each man picked his own coffee, pulped it by hand or in a machine, fermented, washed and dried his own beans. Many trees were dried and neglected. The machines were not integrated with fermenting vats and running water, so that the quality of coffee declined. Most coffee sales were to private buyers; the cooperative had not kept its members or its standards.

Food production and sale is mostly in the hands of the women. This includes carrying vegetables some miles to the government post at Kundiawa once or twice a week for sale. There have been family quarrels over the disposal of the money so earned, but nowadays, with coffee a much larger cash producer, this source of family conflict is probably declining. The peak of expectations of income from market gardening occurred in 1959-60 when Kondom, a leader and entrepreneur, began a project at Bagngitci (Brookfield and Brown 1963: 123-4). The land owners received 20 pigs in payment for the land, and some crops and pigs were raised there, but the enterprise declined to an extension of Kondom's household farms.

There have been a few other small-scale financial opportunities in the area. On some frequently traveled roads, stalls have been set up to sell food. Kondom had a short-lived and rarely active café at Wandi, which was mostly an eating and gathering place for his followers, many of whom worked for him without wages. Some enterprising men employ a few young men or boys as part-time or full-time employees. These are housed, fed and perhaps given a small wage by the employer. A few men worked for the communal coffee processing activities. When a quantity of coffee was sold, they were given a share of the proceeds by each participant.

Trade stores are often begun by a big man with the collection of money from a group of his supporters. Most of the customers are members of the big man's clan segment; his followers help to run the store and carry provisions, and a young man who can write keeps some records. This is a new mode of big man economic and political enterprise. They get labor, funds and service, and their followers enjoy the activity and support of the big man. Literate young men are sometimes called upon to record the payments made at a marriage and quantities and prices when coffee is sold.

In 1965 family cash income varied greatly — nearly all men in Naregu tribe had some coffee trees in production, but I estimate that very few made as much as $100 in 1965. Perhaps one or two percent of the men earned $500 or more, and most of these were big men, with a group of dependents and employees, and often with other enterprises, such as a trade store.

Chapter 16

Local Leadership and Activities

A CHIMBU HAD to compete among his fellows for prominence at every level of social and political grouping. The qualifications for social importance were achievement in technical, political, economic and military activities. Magic, ritual and medical matters were not specialized in Chimbu, and were not an important part of a leader's knowledge. Every man needed technological skill in garden clearing and preparation, house and fence building, pig raising and such manufacturing work as making spears, bows, arrows, bark cloth, belts, armbands, rope, sharpening and repairing stone axes, etc. An important man had a group of followers whose productive activities he directed. This was the basis of his wealth and importance. From this, a man could accumulate pigs, wives, land and valuables, which would permit him to participate widely in exchange relationships. The most successful men used their knowledge of relationships and intergroup ties and abilities in speech-making and in organizing large-scale transactions. They created new ties and relationships in all their fights and exchange transactions with other groups. At all ceremonial occasions they planned, directed, arranged the display and took a leading part in speaking and distributing goods. No man could maintain an important position into very old age, nor could his son simply take over his position. The requirements for a big man included constant adaptation to changing interpersonal and intergroup relations, and active, energetic participation in social, political and economic activities. It also required a large supporting household to provide the goods and basis for his participation.

The new roles of government-created village officials (who have

"brass") were somewhat different from those of traditional big men, but
they did involve some of the same kinds of activity. Most of the big men
I knew in the first years of fieldwork were active organizers of ceremonial
exchanges. They led their groups in feasts, displays and exchange, and
they made speeches at these ceremonial occasions, demonstrating knowledge of intergroup relations. The recognition of a big man depends less
on ability and knowledge in organizing ceremonial activities since the introduction of cash cropping, local government councils, Christianity and
other new areas of interest and achievement. Chimbu *tultuls* and *luluais*,
and later councillors *"konsel"* organize and direct public works ordered
by the government, resolve disputes and take them to the government
court, and encourage people to grow crops for sale.

There were several distinct realms of leadership in the late 1950's. Com-
mitteemen *"komdi"* were in charge of organizing work and services for
the government schools. Selected church members led in prayers and
organized people for work and attendance at mission activities. The educated young men played an important part in local development, because
they were the source of information and skills concerning new technical and
economic activities, as well as knowledge about the white man and his
political and legal rules.

Throughout the changes in political and leadership activites, the role
of big man has continued, although in somewhat different form. A
prominent man has followers who are indebted to him for help in payments
or gifts of land, and support in their relations with others. Frequently,
such dependents are part of the men's house group founded by the leader,
and have their families in residence nearby. They support the big man
by providing services and help for him in building and gardening, and
helping him with food and goods for the payments which he must make to
maintain his position. Although the building materials, kind of crops
grown, kind of goods given in exchange, etc. have all changed over time,
the political and support relationships between leaders and followers have
continued.

The traditional role of the outstanding big man of a clan segment,
composed of a few hundred people, was to organize the local unit in exchanges and in rivalry, to defend it against outsiders seeking land, and to
represent the group in clan and tribal affairs. The first *bosbois* were selected
and given new responsibilities by the administration to report disturbances, take troublemakers to government headquarters, to bring all people
to see the officer on request for a census or for public works, and to pass on
information to members of their groups. The *tultuls* appointed in the early
1950's had usually represented a single subclan, and this was a natural segment for political organization. There were several big men in each clan,
and often one was pre-eminent. But this was not a recognized leadership

level in every Chimbu administration. One big man among these clan leaders was the powerful, impressive and dominant leader of a tribe. His role was validated after the cessation of tribal warfare by organizing large-scale exchanges and pig feasts. The official *luluais* appointed in the 1930's and 1940's were the most promising big men of their tribes, with large land-holdings and considerable followings of wives and attached families.

After about 1950, another pattern of leadership and wealth began to emerge. These were men who were youths in the 1930's, and acquired some new knowledge and skills by being attached to Europeans, some of them going to school, others working as domestics or laborers for European employers. Under the leadership of an enterprising big man, a group of men often pool their money to invest in a coffee-pulping machine, vehicle, shop, or some other new and expensive object which may produce income.

During the 1950's, many aging *luluais* and *tultuls* retired and were replaced by younger men with modernizing interests and skills. Occasionally, the replacements were sons of the former big men, but quite frequently they were younger men with no inherited advantage in achieving their position. In 1958, when I first visited Chimbu, I found some aging, older *luluais* and *tultuls* who were mainly interested in local ceremonies and exchanges, and viewed their official task as carrying out the government orders and taking difficult cases to the government headquarters for trial. There was also quite a considerable group of younger leaders; some were *tultuls* who had replaced the first appointees, while others were active innovators and spokesmen in the many discussions that took place at that time. The government had already proposed introducing local government councils, and there were many meetings and discussions to prepare for this. The main themes expressed in these meetings were an approval of the white man's introduced ways of peace, progress, and support of work, business, schools, councils, improvement of housing and standard of living. People were cautioned to give up stealing, fighting, and marital quarrels, and live peaceably for group improvement. The main avenues to this were commercial crop-growing, especially the development of coffee, and cooperation in cutting planks for new buildings and working on the road to improve transport and communications. In the 1950's and 1960's speakers and leaders expressed their dependence upon and support of the Australian government, which was bringing them all of these opportunities for development.

The institution of the Waiye Native Local Government Council was a considerable reorganization of political groupings in Chimbu. It encompassed four previously autonomous and competitive tribes. The elected representatives elected president and vice presidents from among their group. An entirely new governmental structure and set of procedures was to be understood. The basic requirement for the establishment of a council is the ability of the community to pay a small tax. There has to be some money-making activity in the area, usually some local production. In Chimbu coffee became increasingly the dominant source of income, although there has always been wage labor and some sale of firewood and garden produce. The first *tultuls* had been in charge of social units which the Australian officers thought of local origin, principally subclans, but in many cases not really conforming to the traditional political units. When the new local government council required a larger group as the electorate for a councillor some revision in the groupings took place.

Most of the local government council electoral units had a population of 200-350, often two or three subclans, and this meant that there was often competition between the component subclans for leadership and the council position. Two or three were nominated and the ballot decided the winner. Quite often, in 1959 and 1960, I noticed that the councillor was able to get participation and support from those members of his electorate who were in his own subclan, but not from the members of the other subclan who also formed part of his electorate. This was particularly difficult when he attempted to resolve disputes and conflicts.

The council became a government instrument to make announcements and give instruction to the council members for public works and other kinds of activity. The doctor, Agricultural Officer, Educational Officer, and others would attend council meetings to make speeches and announcements. Sometimes they requested council participation and funding of their projects, such as local medical-aid posts and school buildings. Since they were illiterate, the *konsel* could only base their understanding of their role, power and privileges on statements made by the Australian officers. They received a small stipend. The council also employed a group of constables, who were responsible for peace and order, and occasionally made formal arrests and took cases to the *kiap*. The council was engaged in building a council house, a trucking business and other enterprises, for which they had no knowledge of costs or methods.

During this time, the local people were enthusiastic over the great changes that would take place through a combination of their newly established coffee-growing activities and the council, which was the political demonstration of their stage of progress. Day after day for many months in 1959-60, men were called to work preparing the council site to the neglect of preparing new gardens, buildings, houses and fences. *Konsel*, constables, and *komdi* were in charge of the group activities for progress towards the new way of life. Schools, roads, coffee processing stations and aid posts were proposed and sometimes built. The *konsel* demonstrated by their productive activity, behavior, dress and housing the new way that all people were urged to achieve. To further its goals, the council exercised some illegal sanctions, such as confiscating cards and marbles, and forcing people to work to punish gambling and courting parties which were regarded as frivolous interference with economic development and progress.

Konsel had no training and little instruction in formal procedures, preparation of agenda, or authority and scope of local government. Council meetings became an arena for discussion and speechmaking by leaders. The most prevalent themes were: all people should work, not quarrel, take care of the sick, follow the *kiap's* orders, stop gambling, help one another, develop cash crops, have only one wife, councillors should set an example by not participating in ceremonies, houses should be built in lines and villages established, disputes should be taken to the police, pigs should be kept from going into gardens and destroying crops, there should be payment for roadwork and materials supplied, and weapons should not be carried.

The council very rarely made recommendations, enacted rules, or actually carried out any specific activities. In the council meetings, most of the discussion was concerned with questions, requests, and complaints by the councillors, who wanted more schools, more medical services, higher income, and greater payment for roadwork and other activities. Its functions were to promote unity and progress rather than to accomplish specific governmental tasks.

Nearly all of the older traditional leaders, who had been warriors and later *luluais* and *tultuls,* retired with waning influence in local affairs. Most of them worked and lived as ordinary ageing men. Some of the younger, economically progressive men elected as *konsel* proved to be ineffective leaders, poor speechmakers, and lacking the support of their electorate, so that they did not accomplish much in their new roles. In the first couple of years, there was much shaking down between these new and progressive young leaders, so that the effective speakers and organizers succeeded, and the ineffective ones were not reelected. The leading men of most subclans had a turn as *konsel,* but only the most able kept their office. The council was a showplace, and councillors all attempted to have for themselves the physical and technical symbols of progress. At the same time, some of the groups within the local government council were holding a large pig feast, which was meant to mark the end of traditional ways of feasting and exchanging, and a wholehearted turning to the new ways after the feast was finished. The leading *konsel* attempted to make all people in the council turn completely to new activities and new goals which involved working together, supporting the government schools, learning new skills, and devoting themselves to economic activities, especially coffee-growing. There was some underlying resentment of outsiders in the area, and concern that local people should receive the schooling that would permit them to have skilled jobs, which had until then been held by natives from more developed parts of the territory.

Thus enthusiasm and forced working together could not last, and indeed, it began to drop off about a year after the council was established. Traditional ceremonial activities began to be neglected in favor of commercial activities, but there was widespread disappointment when the world coffee price dropped and the income from coffee did not provide the great things that they had been hoping for. Intertribal antagonisms could not be permanently avoided, but reasserted themselves in various events that took place during and after the feasts.

In the next few years, the people began to adapt to the new way of council government. A great deal of help and attention was required from the Australian officers, who superintended the council and various economic and social matters. The council clerk, a local Chimbu, who had been to a clerical training school, was inadequate to the task. The council engaged in some economic enterprises, but nearly everything was originated by the Australian administrative officers, who recommended ways of investing council income and helped to carry out the arrangements. The *konsel* was a kind of agent of the government among the people: he organized and recruited workers and people to hear when the administration sent information officers among the people, directed all of the public works activities, and continued many of the other functions, such as settling disputes, of the former *tultuls* and *luluais*. Former *tultuls*, local leaders and unsuccessful candidates were *"komdi"* who assisted or took the place of the councillor in local affairs.

The substitution of elected for appointed officials did not greatly change the relationship between the people and the colonial government. A council as inexperienced as Chimbu did not originate laws or new activities, rather the council received suggestions from the Australian administration and attempted to carry them out. The chief complaints of the councillors in their meetings were that they did not have the support and work force of their own council members. The great move for cooperative progress had deteriorated, and economic activity was individualized. Support for public works, schools, agricultural development, and medical work declined. People depended greatly upon the government for information, new techniques, and law and order; but the council was mainly an instrument of the administration. The people asked the government for things; they did not demand them or assign priorities. There was considerable resentment, at this time, of white men, especially of traders, and of the low salaries and payments that they received from the white man. They also did not much improve their standards of living during these years, even though coffee was developing as a larger crop. Many people said that public order, the courts and punishment of offenders, had been better under the *luluais* and *tultuls* than they now were under the council. It was obvious that the council organization had not brought about rapid progress.

While two-thirds of the councillors had been replaced by the third election, there was no training in council procedure and responsibilities, but rather the pattern which had been set in the beginning of council activities continued. Routine matters were discussed repeatedly and endlessly, motions were passed which could not be acted upon, and rules were proposed which would be unenforceable or illegal. Councillors wanted to punish people who did not follow their orders or got into trouble by old-fashioned, traditional kinds of strong-armed methods of force. This was outside their area of jurisdiction. The same mood was shown by this item in a Pidgin English report of the proceedings of the Lowa Council in the Eastern Highlands of New Guinea: *"Kaunsila Huke i bin tok sampela man i no save harim tok bilong kaunsila long wok long rod samting. Em i laik bai Kaunsil i putim rul oa lo bai i mas harim tok bilong kaunsila long wok olosem. Kaunsil bai i asikim nambawan kiap long asikim nambawan long Moresby long givim strong long kaunsil long mekim lo olosem* (Eastern Highlands Councillor 1960:4)."

Freely translated, this means: "Councillor Huke said some men do not obey the councillors' orders about work on the roads and other things. He wants the council to make a rule or law that people must obey the councillors' work orders. He asks the District Commissioner to ask the Administrator in Port Moresby to allow the council to make such a law." It is clear that the councillor recognizes that his authority depends upon the government, and he looks to the government to enforce it.

At my next visit, in 1963, there was more evidence of variation and fluctuation of interests. Economic development was emphasized with almost no public expression of interest in traditional forms of exchange. The colonial officers restrained their influence in local council affairs and stimulated the local people to make policy. The council had as an important decision at that time the question of raising taxes, which would allow them to expand public works investment, but many people felt that they could not afford this higher rate of tax. They were then dependent upon government initiative and demonstration of what would be the likely outcome of such changes. The *konsel* were still frustrated in their inability to command work and support from the people. A local fight which had taken place within the tribe between two groups over the repair of a road, ended in large-scale jailing of the participants.

A comparison of local government councils in neighboring areas, with different Australian officers, shows a very great contrast in morale and in successful activities. Changing Australian administrative officers brought different aims and styles of participation in council decisions. In 1965,

I observed more efficient procedures and an effective committee setting the agenda for meetings.

It is clear that there is no single, simple, direct line of development from one stage to another. Rather, close observaton of a council over a period of years showed that there was initial high enthusiasm, followed, about three years later, with growing apathy, dissatisfaction and a very greatly declined rate of attendance and participation in council affairs. At the same time, individual economic activities were improving. The local leaders were often both councillors and holders of large coffee plots and other enterprises. They inevitably neglected some public or private affairs. Some councillors refused reelection so that they might have time for their own affairs.

In the 1960's, some forms of small local collective activity declined, while individual enterprise and some large group activities expanded. The former network of individual ties was breaking down with the reduction in traditional exchange activities and a concentration on public works and private enterprise. There was an acceptance of inclusive administrative institutions, with a growing awareness of the large-scale Australian colonial power as responsible for progress. Chimbus were not satisfied with their achievements, or with the people's support of the new goals.

During these years the same dominant theme appeared at all public meetings and discussions — the leaders want progress in the form of coffee production, schools, health services, and improved standard of living, but the people are lazy and uncooperative. The council has no sanctions to force a change.

Neither the council nor any other form of organization or activity was self-sustaining during this period: councils met and people came to meetings or to public works projects on the orders of the Australian officers. Since there was much discussion on the national level of preparation for self-government, I sometimes asked what would happen if the Australians left. Some men replied, " We have our *konsel, komdi,* and constables; they would carry on." But the possibility was not taken seriously.

In the next years, 1966 and later, a combined council was formed to bring together Kundiawa town and several local councils. This required a reduction in the number of councillors to approximately one for each clan, a separation of the council from local affairs, and governmental activity of a broader scope. The participation of local people inevitably declined as the size of the council increased. However in 1971 my brief visit gave me a view of a new development: Chimbu leaders and followers could function in a variety of roles and activities, and could move readily from one to another. They were integrating both traditional and new skills and behavior in a most sophisticated way.

Chapter 17

Conflict Today

CHANGING ECONOMIC and social circumstances in the Chimbu area have not reduced the frequency of conflict. When fighting is eliminated as a means of reacting to conflict, then other traditional means, such as threat or suspicion of sorcery, may increase, or new modes of dealing with conflict, such as mediation, may appear. The more permanent and stable settlements, with large gardens, more pigs and more people, and the consequent reduction in the movements of people, may bring about a higher rate of conflict. Inheritance of improved land, trees and houses is more important, and property is more closely guarded. The increase in quantity and variety of property, the uneven growth of wealth, may tempt more thieves. Monogamy, with the traditional long tabu on sexual relations after childbirth, may lead to more adultery and other sexual offenses than the previous conditions which allowed polygyny. Wider ties and contact with strangers may stimulate an increase in sorcery beliefs and accusations. The introduction of card gambling games has been accompanied by fights between players and over debts. The introduction of coffee as a tree crop makes land encroachment and crop damage by pigs a serious threat to income. The introduction of new, costly and valued varieties of pigs, dogs, chickens and ducks has also made the loss or theft of livestock a serious offense. These increasing concerns for property make conflict at least as likely and perhaps more common than in pre-contact days: people have more to lose, and less opportunity to regain losses by self-help.

Probably the one regulation that has had the greatest impact on native life is the suppression of fighting and warfare by the Australian administration. This was the first concern of government officers, and the main responsibility of native officials, especially in the early years. Small personal quarrels and fights were stopped by local officials so that they would not become inter-group fights. When they did become inter-group fights, the government officer was notified and a combined force of native police and local natives intervened to stop it and punish the instigators. The Australian administration has tried to stop any outward show of conflict, making of weapons, using bows and arrows, spears, knives, clubs, etc. against other people, and has endeavored to stop fights once they began. But this does not prevent conflicts and disputes from arising, or determine that they will be resolved by some peaceful means. Indeed, the most difficult part of pacification is convincing the litigants to accept a court judgment and punishment as the solution to conflict.

The Australian officers stationed in the Chimbu area mentioned in their reports of 1935 to 1940 that many men were sent to jail for riotous behavior, assault or killing. The precipitating cause of the conflict was rarely investigated. Upon his release from jail, a man bore the same grievance that provoked him to fight in the first place and he often attempted to regain his property or restore his rights by a further show of force. The significant question then, is: How are conflicts resolved when fighting is prevented and sentencing to a period in jail simply removes the immediate cause of disturbance for a period? Tempers may quiet down but does this mean that the dispute is resolved? Or does the grievance simmer until a further occasion of conflict bursts into another fight?

In any small community, over time, there are many grudges and grievances which may be suddenly brought into the open by an immediate conflict. Whenever I attempted to trace back the source of a quarrel, I found that there were many precipitating incidents of disagreement between the parties or the groups in the quarrel. In pre-contact times, such suppressed, continuous hostility between groups would, from time to time, break out in fighting or raids, sometimes satisfying one party by the theft of a pig or a quick retaliation, but producing a pervading sense of competition and hostility between groups at all levels within and between tribes.

Fighting alternated with peacemaking and exchange of goods, food and valuables between the clans or tribes. Fighting has not been entirely eliminated, but it cannot be of any duration, since the fighters are stopped by other local people, or police are called in, and then are brought to the government post for punishment. A fight which developed between two clans within Naregu tribe in 1963 led to the jailing of a number of men on both sides for three months, and the requirement of a £2 fine from each man. After the jail sentence was completed, they planned a peacemaking pig feast to reestablish normal relations and the prestige of the group.

However, the move towards cash economy prevented the full expression of this, and it was years before the whole tribe coordinated its efforts.

Most conflicts remain inter-personal, and are aired, discussed, and sometimes resolved first locally, by a combination of interested parties and the native officials. Before 1959, *luluais* and *tultuls* took the lead in discussing and attempting to resolve dispute cases. Since 1959, *konsels* and other leaders, such as *komdi,* have held "court" on dispute cases. Council constables sometimes heard cases or brought offenders to the government station. The parties occasionally come to blows or raise a general cry, alarm or complaint. Then the nearest native officials call together the disputing parties and witnesses for a *kot* ("court"). Sometimes not all parties appear, or other issues prevent full discussion of the case, and it is deferred to another time, or never held. Quite often, the initial discussion and public airing satisfies the complainant with the assumption of wrong, and sometimes claim for compensation.

In a clear-cut situation, such as discovery in the act of theft or adultery, or the admission of debt, restitution or payment of damages is immediately claimed and, if the responsible party is able to do so, paid on the spot. But most of the time the case is by no means so definitive, and the parties are unable to agree upon responsibility or the amount of compensation to be paid.

In the cases I heard discussed, a restitution or compensation was hardly ever claimed and paid. Quite frequently, the leading men assigned responsibility and instructed the guilty or wrong party to pay, but he usually excused himself by inability to pay at that time. Only an anthropologist would follow up such a case — and by doing so I found I might influence the proceedings. I rarely discovered whether payment had been made. And from the frequency of second, third, fourth, etc. hearings of the same case, with often some new development, it was obvious that restitution was very rarely paid. Many complainants had only the satisfaction of the publicity and public assignment of guilt to another party.

Table III summarizes cases I observed in the Mintima area, with some notes on compensation or resolution when it was observed.

An extremely common form of dispute is that concerning a pig who pushed through a fence and into a garden, destroying some part of a crop. This has always been a frequent occurrence, and in such instances, the garden owner may take matters into his own hands and capture, or sometimes kill, and eat the pig. Such could, in the past, have been the cause of a large fight, especially if the garden damage is by no means equal to the value of the pig, and the pig and garden were the property of members of different tribes or clans. Nowadays, it is much more common for the garden owner to raise a complaint and request compensation from

TABLE III   Dispute Cases Discussed in Court with Native Leaders

Interpersonal:	Number of Cases
Claim for payment or reallocation of payment at death	8
Debts and payments between tribes	2
Gambling quarrel over payment of losses	2
Membership in group, adoption and residence	2
Marital quarrel, beating or fighting — discussed	7
Payment made to resolve (2)	
Divorce — return some of marriage payment	6
Separation — told to remain together	7
Divorcée and remarriage	1
Adultery and suspected adultery	3
(In one case, compensation paid to husband £5)	
Widow marriage — Widow refuses	6
— Widow chooses outside husband's group	2
Quarrels between women	5
Complaint against woman in group — lazy, quarrelsome	1
Father forcing daughter's marriage	1
Infanticide accusation by husband of wife	1
Burial place of man who died of feared disease	1
Accusation of killing by sorcery	4
Fighting among children	2
(In one case, parents fought and council	
president ordered them to hard labor)	
Quarrel between man and his brother's wife — discussed	1
Indecent approach to young girl — compensation demanded	1
Land:	
Rights to trees	2
Land encroachment or conflict of claims	6
Widow's right to husband's land	1
Rights to coffee trees	3
Trespass	1
Theft of food, goods or money — compensation or	
restitution demanded	6
Theft accusation and insult	1
Killed dog that attacked chickens	2
(In one case, paid)	
Pigs:	
Pigs damage gardens:	
Garden owner claims compensation and	
payment given or promised	6
Pig killed or intent to kill	4
No damage assigned	4
Outcome not determined	3
Quarrel over sale of pig	1
Quarrel between brothers over care of pig	1
Divorce and repayment of pigs	1
Lost or strayed pigs	2
TOTAL DISPUTE CASES:	107

the pig's owner. This is sometimes the cause of a subsidiary conflict between a man and his wife over responsibility for controlling the pig or keeping it adequately fed so that it does not enter gardens and damage crops. The pig's owner is sometimes told to compensate the garden owner with money, but in fact he usually claims that he has no money and the matter drops. Sometimes a group is ordered by the native official to repair the damage in the fence so as to prevent further intrusions by pigs into gardens. Occasionally, the general view is that the pig is a vicious and dangerous animal, and its owner or someone else is required to kill it.

When the parties in a dispute could neither agree nor allow their complaints to be dismissed and the native official could find no solution, he frequently took the case to some higher authority. In the Naregu tribe, for many years, these cases were taken to Kondom, the *luluai* and later the council president. Throughout my period of field work, Kondom was the acknowledged chief justice of Naregu. On certain days, when he was known to be at home at Wandi holding his *kot,* he often had several cases pending at once. Small groups of people, who had been in an insoluble quarrel, were brought from all parts of Naregu tribal territory to Wandi by the *konsel* and *komdi,* in order that the cases could be discussed and perhaps settled. Kondom's hearings were assisted by the *konsel* and *komdi* of the parties involved. He disentangled claims and accusations, questioned witnesses or interested parties, and arrived at some assessment of the rights of the case. Kondom's *kot,* like those of *tultuls* and *konsel,* were often inconclusive. He usually told the people to go home and stop quarreling, and at other times he told them to make some sort of compensation or recompense, and then when the person told to make a payment claimed that he was unable to do so, the case was simply set aside. There was no record of the decision or any payment made. There was no way in which Kondom's rules could be enforced. Frequently, local knowledge and publicity was a satisfying procedure for the disputants, and this was as far as the case would be carried. There was a brief period, during the building of the council house and preparation of the council site, in which people who had been caught disobeying council orders were put to work in what was known as the local *kalabus,* carrying rocks and earth to make a more level area. Young people who engaged in forbidden courting parties were especially likely to be sentenced to local *kalabus.*

At a later date, in about 1964, there was another innovation, involving the use of the constables and *konsel* from a different area than that of the disputants. Several of these were regarded as especially good adjudicators, and were called to hear and discuss disputes between people of tribes other than their own. This procedure never lasted very long, and seemed to be especially indecisive, with no possible enforcement. My notes over the years indicate a general decline in all kinds of cases discussed on the local level between councillors and tribesmen. I think this indicates a trend. As the Chimbu became more accustomed to the circumstances of Australian administration, they were less often vigorously involved in quarrels, and assault and violence were in fact less frequent. At the beginning of my period of field work, and for some years previously, leaders of the Chimbus had continuously exhorted the people to stop quarreling and fighting among one another, to live peacefully together and work together for progress. This seems to have in fact occurred, perhaps as much from the dissatisfaction in solutions to disputes as from the positive desire to live a calmer and more peaceful life. There are also some new modes of avoiding strife, by temporary or permanent migration to work in a different area. Yet intergroup fighting continues to occur now and then, when conflict develops. The Chimbu have not changed their character or their propensity to violence in anger.

Several sorts of disputes found their way to the government officer in his role as magistrate — the *kiap's* court at the government station. Matters involving serious injury, assault, death, or intergroup fighting, which are well known to be against the law, were regularly brought to Kundiawa and fairly promptly heard and sentenced by a government officer in charge. Others were too difficult for the local *konsel* and *komdi* to decide. Table IV shows a sample of cases from the Mintima area which were taken to the *kiap* during my field work.

TABLE IV   Cases Taken from Local Discussion to Government Office
for Hearing

Adultery	3
Intertribal death payment fight	1
Accidental killing of boy, followed by retaliation, killing	1
Marital quarrel, wife kills husband with axe	1
Quarrel over pig, debt — killings; 3 months' jail	1
Interclan fight — all fighting men jailed 3 months	1
Intertribal land dispute — weapons prepared	1
Gambling — council constable confiscates — arrests	1
Divorce and repayment	4
Elopement	1
TOTAL	**15**

There was a period of about two years, 1959-60, during which the council attempted to suppress gambling in the form of a card game called lucky. This game was always illegal, but had rarely been punished. The council constables who caught men playing lucky confiscated the cards and money, and took them into court. When I went over the cases heard by the Court of Native Affairs in 1959 and 1960 (Table V), I found a large number of gambling cases and recorded only a few of them, since they were highly repetitive. There were also many cases involving station employees, and these I did not fully record either.

TABLE V   Cases in Court of Native Affairs and Native Matters, 1959-60
(*Sample — partly random, partly selected from Kundiawa area.*)

Cases	number		per cent
Offenses against administration orders	12	20	11.4
Offenses against administration, gambling	8		
Offenses involving officials:			
against authority of official	4	9	5.1
misuse of authority of official	5		
Sorcery and assault, homicide	8	9	5.1
Magic dispute, assault	1		
Property:			
theft, property	21		
theft and fights over property accusation	9		
fights over pig theft, accusation	14	47	26.8
destruction of house	2		
insult and fight	1		
Sex and marriage:			
agnatic control over women	5		
affines	3		
marriage payment, fight	7		
sexual jealousy, fight between men or			
between women	4		
sexual insult (women)	1		
pretended cure of barrenness, adultery	1		
sexual offenses (young girl)	9	90	51.4
prostitution (government station)	4		
intercourse with foster daughter	1		
marital quarrel, assault	13		
false report of incest and adultery	4		
adultery	25		
adultery and assault	7		
adultery attempt, accusation	6		
TOTAL:	175		99.8

In Kundiawa, at the Court of Native Affairs heard by the patrol officer or assistant district officer, the procedure was, on the whole, informal. The native official, *tultul* or *konsel* often went first to a government policeman or interpreter and explained the case to him. Then they together often sent the parties away or suggested a solution, so that the dispute never reached the Australian officer. The selection of cases in Table V shows that only certain kinds of cases were likely to be discussed in the Court of Native Affairs. The *kiap* acting as magistrate used an interpreter to hear the case in Pidgin English translated from Chimbu. A brief record was made of the case, and a judgment usually resulted in a term of less than three months in prison. In comparison with the cases heard locally, the cases heard in the Court of Native Affairs have a higher proportion of assault and injury cases, thefts, false reports, and are on the whole more to be classified as criminal cases than as civil cases. Civil cases that come before the court frequently involve violence over a personal conflict of interest. The cases are on the whole more serious than those involving a discussion of conflicting claims for payment or claims over land. It is, after all, the resistant cases which come all the way to the government station. Only the *kiap* can sentence a person to *kalabus;* the *konsel's kot* may recommend restitution or payment.

A good many of the cases heard in the Court of Native Affairs involve station residents and employees: natives from other parts of the territory and Europeans who have no mediators among their own group. They must use government officers. Cases involving gambling and offenses against administration orders are of course typical of the special circumstances of the Court of Native Affairs.

While station employees fairly often had money to pay fines that were imposed by a court order, the local Chimbus rarely had money with which they could pay fines. The typical judgment was a short prison sentence. While serving his sentence, a Chimbu lived in a large general dormitory building in the government station, and was given food rations and clothing by the government. *Kalabus* prisoners did some work on the roads or grounds of the government station. The position of a prisoner could hardly be said to be one of great discomfort or suffering. In fact, in later years, the local officials believed that prison was much too easy for people sentenced, the food and clothing better than that of local Chimbus, and pleaded for harsher treatment of criminals. Since the only threat that a native official had against people who disobeyed him and government orders was to take him to the *kiap* who would send them to *kalabus,* the fact that the *kalabus* was not as unpleasant as they may have wished was hardly an enforcement of their authority.

A still higher court than the Court of Native Affairs is the Supreme Court, which circulates throughout the territory with a Supreme Court Judge, meeting at government stations on circuit. Particularly serious cases, involving serious assaults, death and large thefts, are reserved for hearing by the Supreme Court judges. The culprit was frequently known and immediately seized, and held in jail awaiting trial. Such cases were very few in any district. Court procedure was very much more exact and formal, involving a court recorder, and interpretation from Chimbu to Pidgin, and Pidgin to English, and of course back again whenever a witness or defendant was questioned. Most of the cases in Chimbu were murders of relatives over a quarrel, adultery, witchcraft accusation. The sentence of death was usually commuted to a term of imprisonment.

A special and distinct development of a Lands Commission for inter-group territorial disputes and land cases was instituted in the territory. The Lands Commissioner investigates specific land disputes as individual cases, usually on the spot, often in an inquiry involving members of several tribes. The decisions are fully written out and form the basis of territorial demarcations. Hearings are held at the place of dispute and often involve many days or weeks of discussion of rights, claims, and history of occupancy. Land demarcation procedures are discussed by Hide (1971).

The system of dispute settlement and criminal prosecution found in New Guinea is distinctively different from that in many other colonial territories. Papua New Guinea has no formal body of law adapted to local conditions, and it has no official indigenous system of courts and judges empowered to enforce sanctions. The whole system is taken from Australia and exercised by Australian judges and magistrates. Only recently have New Guineans been trained in the law and national and local bodies given legislative power.

Chapter 18

Kondom's Kingdom

DURING THE 1960's Chimbus began to see more of the world outside the highlands. Councillors and students attended meetings and teaching programs. They were increasingly aware of the differences between themselves and others, and of the complexity of skills and knowledge needed for them to reach their goals.

The initial combination of leadership and progress can be shown in this summary sketch of the Naregu and Chimbu leader, Kondom, who died in a car accident in 1966.

Kondom was an outstanding personality and by his energy, example and precept led the Chimbu from a collection of fighting tribes to peaceable members of the Chimbu Coffee Cooperative and participants in local and territorial government. His driving force took up the potential of the time and propelled it further than the normal pace of development might have done.

Kondom must have been born between 1917 and 1920; my personal acquaintance with him was from 1958 to 1965. His boyhood was, as typically in Chimbu, a time of intertribal fighting. His father Agaundo died young, leaving Kondom to be attached to various relatives — his paternal kinsmen at Wandi about three miles from Kundiawa, and his maternal relatives across the Singga river to the north in hostile territory.

Chimbu got its first government post and mission when Kondom was still a boy. Father Schaefer began the Catholic mission at Mingende in 1934. Kondom was one of their first milk boys, but he never became a Catholic. A little later he was at the Chimbu post in Kundiawa, mostly, I gathered, working on gardens. He had no schooling and no training in any trade; as far as I know he was not employed by Europeans after this time. By 1940 the Chimbu area was more or less considered pacified. A number of *luluais* had been appointed, including Arime of Naregu, Kondom's tribe. Arime was a traditional big man who became more attached to the church than to the government. Angered because he was given a bullock by the mission and nothing by the administration, he did not bring his tribe out for work or census. Arime was dismissed sometime in the early 1940's. ANGAU records in Chimbu for this period have not survived. My next source, a report for 1945, lists Kondom as the *luluai* of Naregu tribe.

In the early 1940's, Kondom must have been a prominent young man, energetic and greatly interested in the white man's goods and behavior. His gifts as an orator and leader may already have been evident, and he early began to accumulate wives and followers. At different times Kondom had seven to eleven women attached to him and a varying number of men who were younger members of his local clan and tribe, brothers-in-law and simply hired workers. My record is incomplete but I believe there were more than sixteen children, some of them adopted.

Kondom can have seen little beyond Chimbu until after 1950, for Kundiawa had a small staff and communications were limited. It was still rare for highland natives to leave their tribal territory. The road to Goroka was completed in 1953. From the early 1950's, Kondom expanded his activities in many directions. Chimbu men were signing up as agreement laborers, some government schools were begun and coffee plantings were being established. Kondom spent much of his time at Kundiawa, met and spoke with as many Australian officials as he could. At every opportunity he pressed for Chimbu development and urged the building of schools, meeting houses, medical aid posts and the introduction of cash crops. He was among the first to plant coffee and showed other Chimbus how to do it. A coffee pulper was acquired as soon as the first trees bore fruit. Wandi, on the main road three miles from Kundiawa, became a Government Rest House site after Kondom was *luluai*, and his development a display site with coffee trees, the coffee pulper and a meeting house.

In 1954, a series of bi-weekly and later monthly meetings were instituted in a large hall he built at Wandi. The first meetings encouraged the planting of coffee, passion fruit, peanuts and other European vegetables, with the aim of selling to European residents and buyers at the government station. Kondom was joined by some leaders from neighboring tribes and the *tultuls* of his own tribe to discuss economic and other matters, sometimes with the native affairs officers. For the most part, Kondom made speeches and laid down rules and programs for development. Here is a text translated from a notebook in Pidgin:

My name is *Luluai* Kondom. The meeting is about the government laws. I want the natives to hold these laws. These are the rules:

1. Men must not kill other human beings.
2. Men must not commit adultery with young girls and old women.
3. Men must not burn the houses.
4. Men must not steal someone's property.
5. Men must listen to their headman or *luluai* or *tultul*.
6. The women must not kill the newborn infant.
7. A man must not commit adultery with someone's wife.
8. The best and most important one is education.

It was emphasized that breaking any of these rules would bring the miscreants to court. The officers at the time recognized Kondom's ability and enthusiasm for the government, but also noticed his occasional use of coercion. Kondom often adjudicated disputes and sometimes directed a penalty, usually the payment by the offender to the injured party. His interests and activities even at that time were not limited to his own tribe.

Kondom was also a leader in traditional Chimbu activities. He organized the pig feast given by Naregu tribe in 1955-1956 into a very large one which also brought visitors from distant places to admire the display of wealth, pigs and feathers.

Kondom's range of influence grew. Persons in other tribes often consulted him about disputes or plans, and with administration support he attended the District Advisory Council and other meetings as an observer. Most of the other Chimbu *luluais* were aging traditional big men; Kondom was outstanding as a young man with progressive interests. By 1958, he had considerable experience as a government official. He spoke with authority to the people of the government's intentions and impressed the government with his ability to bring his people's support for economic and political progress. He represented the Chimbu Sub-District in the District Advisory Council, was an observer at the Legislative Council in Port Moresby and at the South Pacific Commission's conference in Rabaul.

In 1958, a series of meetings to discuss local government were held in the four tribes which later became the Waiye Council. They followed much the same pattern with an agenda and notes kept by Kambua, a former school teacher. We quote from the blackboard on which the agenda was listed, translating from Pidgin:

1. The story of our work, before, now and in the future.
2. Find out the opinions of men — which men want meetings and which men don't want meetings.
3. Talk about work for the school.
4. Talk about taxes.

5. Talk about work for business.
6. Talk about the council.
7. Talk about fighting.

On other occasions somewhat different agenda were set out: the questions of using medical services, pigs getting into gardens, and women marrying men from distant places were included in some meetings.

At these intertribal gatherings many speeches were made encouraging hard work, especially in planting cash crops and growing coffee, and also promoting peace and goodwill between people and among the tribes, with a promise of wealth and success in the future if all worked together. It was a prelude to the Native Local Government Council which was instituted in early 1959. Kondom was always in the forefront making the most impressive speeches, but he had the support of many leaders from his own and other tribes.

In his public role Kondom used political techniques comparable to those of the best statesmen. He had met Prince Philip on a visit to New Guinea; he frequently quoted the conversation that they had and his discussions with other important officers. These conversations were said to be responsible for the present and future achievements of the Chimbu, the introduction of schools, the development of coffee, and the Local Government Council. Thus Kondom was regarded as a culture hero who brought progress to Chimbu.

In his speeches to European audiences, Kondom often said, "I am ignorant and uneducated, you are wise and must show me what to do." In his speeches to the Chimbu, he said, "The government tells us what work to do, we must work hard." When disappointed with the effort Chimbus made he harangued and exhorted them and occasionally threatened them or called them backward and bigheaded.

Throughout, the relations that he had with Europeans were very important to him. It was from these conversations that the ideas, plans and practices which he tried to put into effect in Chimbu developed. In my first week there one of the large tribal meetings was held, and since I thought I would find the distant walk across the country too tiring, he assigned two strong men the task of carrying me part of the way so that I could attend with him. I was a kind of trophy belonging to the Naregu tribe.

At this time a tribal enterprise involved the cutting and sawing of timber planks which were to be used for a house for Kondom himself and also for some of the school buildings. He utilized the situation for political, technical and economic encouragement, teaching men to haul logs and saw planks, calling meetings at the building site so that those who attended the meeting would see the construction of a timber house with a corrugated iron roof right in their own territory. He called people together to discuss a number of different points. One of them was about the schools. A few boys of Chimbu were then going to advanced primary school in Goroka and also there was a small government primary school at Wandi. His complaint on this occasion was that the parents of the children in this local school did not bring food for the children or for the teachers. He was also concerned at this time with sickness as there had been an epidemic and many deaths. He wanted improvement in hygiene, use of medical services, and also to give up the old custom of large funeral payments and food distributions as they were becoming a strain on local food supplies. He further discussed taxes and the necessity of paying taxes when Local Government Councils were established. Another item was the lack of full co-operation in the plank-cutting operation that was then taking place. He ended up with, as usual, a work program: "On Monday always go and clean your coffee beds. On Tuesday always 'broom' the big road. Everybody should come out and work on the planks and timber cutting." Kondom said that he would sell his coffee and buy food with the money. "When my house is finished, all the people will come and meet and eat close to the new house." This grand style of entertainment was his ideal, having elements of both Chimbu and the white man's display of wealth and generosity.

The style set the pattern for most of Kondom's activities. He built the first iron-roofed timber house in his tribe and later a stone house. Kondom also built a café with a cement floor, the only one in the area for some years. It was greatly admired but a financial failure. His own domestic organization gave him extensive gardens, many pigs and a great deal of coffee. When he thought that the local coffee traders were giving him an insufficient price for his coffee beans, he invited coffee traders from outside the Chimbu area to come and buy coffee, hoping to get a better price in this way.

As *luluai* and later as president of the Waiye Local Government Council, Kondom was tireless in maintaining peace and order within his tribe. He personally climbed over every part of the territory to investigate problems and encourage progress. He dealt with disputes on the spot and used the occasion further to lecture on the values of peace and hard work and progress. Once in the course of a lecture at Mintima when I was living in the house there, he strolled to my vegetable storage shelf, picked out some undersized tomatoes and said, "What do mean by selling the missus these dirty little tomatoes? These are for chickens, throw them away and grow good vegetables for sale." Most of his speeches finished with a work program of which a very substantial part was the production of goods for sale and income. Many of his speeches included a review of the history of Chimbu from the time when Taylor first entered the area through the end of tribal fighting to the beginning of a council with a great emphasis upon the fact that they are taught by Australians: the mission, the government, the doctor and business have all come to Chimbu to help them.

In 1959, shortly after the Local Government Council was established and before its meeting house was built, he ordered all of the men of the council, all four tribes that is, to work regularly to level and prepare the site. Most of the work was done by men of the Naregu tribe, many of the men working several days a week. Kondom indeed was the boss of the Naregu and to some considerable extent he was also the boss of other groups within the Waiye Council area.

When the Waiye Council was established, a provision was made by the administration officer for the appointment of one councillor so that Kondom was assured of a place on the council. He was repeatedly elected president and his title throughout the area was "President." Later, when he became the member of the Legislative Council, he was regularly called "Masta President." At first he had no idea of council procedures and required much guidance in conducting meetings. The main activity of the council in early years was to hear statements and requests from Kundiawa officers for tax expenditures. The councillors asked questions but did not initiate any action; the local officers made suggestions and proposals.

The first year of the Local Government Council was a time of great enthusiasm for progress. Old customs were discarded and much effort was put into coffee and other cash crop production, the development of the school and the council sites. At this time expectations were very high. The impetus to political and economic progress was combined with a decline of interest in traditional activities and ceremonies. Kondom initiated a large development in an unused portion of tribal territory. Over 200 acres were fenced with strong posts cut by members of Naregu and Nauru tribes, and a bullock team was hired from Mingende mission to plow about ten acres of it. It was to be a cash crop activity, including tobacco and oranges, mostly his own enterprise but also to stand as a model to be copied by other people. Part of the same area was to be used as a cattle pasture for council land. Kondom was showing the way in the development of new economic activities for the Chimbu. But he had led the people to expect a great deal very quickly.

In 1961 Kondom had his greatest success. In the expanded Legislative Council, he was the elected member for the Eastern, Western and Southern Highlands — an unprecedented position for an uneducated tribal leader. He began to regularly fly to Port Moresby, was a member of a group visiting Australia, and was often away from his home area. He no longer toured the tribe to make speeches but he hoped at that time that his example would be followed by hard work throughout. He became remote from the people and was in less contact with everyday matters in the area. His personal experiences were creating a gap between himself and the local people. He described his trip to Australia to the local people telling them: "I went to Brisbane and then to Sydney by plane. There are millions of people in Sydney, it is a big place full of people. The ground is made of cement, the houses are made of brick, there are elevators and the door opens by itself, then you go up. You go to a restaurant for food, you eat meat, fish and rice. The food is all made in a machine. There are houses with a hundred stories — they go up to the clouds. When you eat you sit at a table with plates and have very good food. The Australians have good gardens and good flower gardens. They do not fight and they do not kill their birds. They are friends with all other countries." He ended up with a message, of course. "The Australians teach us, they lift us up. The Australian fashion is number one, it is the best." He also showed slides and photographs from Australia, but nearly all of this was beyond the comprehension of most of the people in his audience. Kondom left the Chimbu behind.

By 1962, a wave of discouragement, bordering on apathy, had taken over. Coffee prices dropped, the educational, medical and agricultural services were little used, no native judiciary was developed and resentments against the Europeans were beginning to be voiced. Kondom's own agricultural scheme had produced an unsuccessful tobacco crop and was largely given over to pigs and sweet potatoes.

In a meeting I attended, the old former *luluais* said, "When we were in office, we told people what to do and they did it. Everyone came to meetings and everyone worked. Now that we have the council, people are big-head, they play lucky and they do not listen to anyone. The *luluais* were the ones who made people work, the councillors don't do anything." It seemed to me that during this period the council had become an instrument of the administration; it was a platform for official announcements. Kondom was used as a go-between from the government to the people. The Chimbu did not seem to have found the road to advancement that Kondom had led them to expect. Many older leaders were becoming tired and discouraged. Kondom continued as President of the Local Government Council but with noticeably less attention and enthusiasm. The 1962 council election saw the replacement of some now experienced councillors with new men. Also, it was clear that some council legislation was ineffective. The council had voted a limitation on marriage payments, but payments continued to increase. Government-sponsored programs were not supported by the people themselves. My own view is that Kondom began to find himself inadequate to the requirements of the new situation.

In this period he seemed to me to be bewildered by the requirements of the position he had attained. His Pidgin English was, I think, inadequate for the job of member of the Legislative Council and the affairs of the Legislative Council were beyond his comprehension. His interests continued to center on local affairs and economic development. The national issues that aroused his attention were the treatment of prisoners, wage scales, roads, agricultural development and land problems. At home he was still full of ideas — ideas on how to sell coffee, coffee processing and machines, cash cropping, nutrition and new types of housing and village planning. He did not convey the Legislative Council affairs to his electorate. In fact, the local people had hardly any idea of the central government and Kondom was unable to explain it.

However, in 1963 he informed the Chimbu of the forthcoming House of Assembly elections and made many explanatory speeches leading up to the elections in 1964. He explained the constitution of the electorates, the form of nomination, and voting procedures. As far as the people in Kondom's tribe were concerned, his nomination was a matter of course, but his political leadership for the larger area was waning. Eleven candidates were nominated, including four others in the Waiye Council area. Although Naregu tribesmen were confident that he would win, he had too much competition in nearby tribes and failed to win sufficient votes from more distant ones. The role of the council in Port Moresby meant little to the Chimbus.

In February 1964, the elections in Chimbu attracted less attention than the organization of Chimbu Coffee Co-operative. Kondom was one of the largest subscribers as the project was very dear to him. He had for years urged the establishment of a native-owned coffee factory and also the development of retail shops. He campaigned vigorously for co-operative membership during the time that election preparations were under way. When the board of directors of the Kundiawa Coffee Co-operative met in April, 1964, Kondom was made chairman and from then on for the rest of his life his chief interest was in the management of the co-operative

Freed of the responsibilities of the Legislative Council, Kondom's local activities blossomed. He was present at the organization of Chimbu branch of the Farmers' and Settlers' Association in 1965 and continued to encourage improvement of coffee planting and processing.

By 1965 the Local Government Council, especially those members who had been active for several years, had become quite sophisticated. As President, Kondom accepted motions and directed the procedure in a highly efficient manner. Members of the council proposed items for the agenda and spoke upon those matters which interested them. They directed communications and inquiries to be sent to officials throughout New Guinea when agricultural, educational, medical, etc. matters were of concern to them.

While being procedurally more efficient, Kondom continued in many of his now habitual ways. He made speeches explaining the laws of the world and the history of government to the people. He said "the law comes from England, then it comes to Canberra to the House of Parliament and from there it comes to New Guinea. I have told the government in Port Moresby what I want but they won't listen to me. They can't change these things in New Guinea, it rests in Canberra." Although he had some of his own views on how the law should be changed, he enthusiastically supported the Australian administration in most of its activities. When blanket weaving and pyrethrum growing were proposed as new economic enterprises, he was very pleased. Procedurally, he was now a master of council work. He would stop people from discussing a matter after a motion had been passed and explain to them what he was doing and why. He had become a good-natured elder statesman, especially inclined to interpretation of the government and of official matters to the people.

Kondom's decline as Chimbu leader began in the 1964 House of Assembly election. A single member was to represent some 40,000 or 50,000 people in the Chimbu valley area. The main loyalties were tribal and regional. Eleven candidates were nominated, and election was by preferential ballot. But little was done to prepare electors or candidates to participate in the new form of government. There was very little activity or campaigning in the Chimbu valley area, and all of the people in the section where I lived automatically supported Kondom and expected that he would be elected. They were most surprised when they found that a man from another area was the chosen person. He succeeded mainly, I think, because he had no competition in his census district. His leadership was short-lived and unremembered.

In the days before the Pax Australiana, no Chimbu could become influential or lead a group larger than a tribe of a few thousand people — rivalry and strife characterized the relations between Chimbu tribes. Kondom came from this tradition; he was a spectacular tribal leader, planning ceremonies and directing activities within Naregu tribe. With the cessation of intertribal fighting, the development of communications, the introduction of developmental projects and the appointment of native officials, the position of *luluai* encompassed responsibilities unknown by former big men: stopping fights and settling quarrels, mobilizing men and women for public works projects, getting popular support for the new administration. Kondom's enthusiasm, energy and oratory made him an outstanding *luluai*. He went on to greater accomplishments — became familiar with organizational procedures so that he was a highly effective president of the Native Local Government Council and chairman of the Chimbu Coffee Co-operative. Throughout, he encouraged the people to support Australian-sponsored activities and urged them to hard work and economic and political progress. He was the main force in bringing schools, cash, medical aid and local government to the region. His travels and meetings with Europeans were a great source of ideas. He was tireless in his efforts to obtain for Chimbu the development he had seen and heard about. Kondom's name stands as a symbol of the beginning of unity and progress in the New Guinea highlands.

But leadership is not the sole factor in understanding the variations in development. Two neighboring electorates had strikingly different elections. Kundiawa, which included the Waiye Council, Dom, Yonggamugl and the Upper Chimbu valley, had eleven candidates, some from the same tribe. The Koro valley area was kept distinct from the Chimbu near Kundiawa. Kerowagi had four candidates who toured the whole area and the election was thoroughly organized for each group to vote at a particular time and place. Only 44% of the eligible voters did vote in the Kundiawa area, while 83% of the eligible voters went to the polls in Kerowagi. At this time, complexity and diversity of interests and activities was most noticeable. There was a wide range of Australian influences and newly created activities to take the time and energy of the local people. The Chimbu Coffee Co-operative was being organized in 1964; the Women's Club began teaching many new skills and activities; and there were some highly specialized activities, such as peanut-growing and a nutritional project for children, blanket-weaving, and a number of new cash crops. The Agriculture Department proposed a scheme for resettlement of some Chimbus. Traditional ceremonies — a pig feast in one of the areas not too far from the local council area, and some other food exchanges involving both traditional goods and purchased foods — were actively continuing. This diversity and range of interests permitted the private support of people with a huge diversity of concerns. It was a time in which individual entrepreneurs could thrive, and group political enterprise seemed to be at a low point.

The alternatives were too many — everyone could not participate in everything. Choices need to be made, and specific goals pursued. In all of this development, certain leaders began to stand out as being skillful and able to deal with the modes of political activity available to them under the circumstances at that time.

Siwi, the member of the House of Assembly from Kerowagi electorate, has become a most important highlands representative, the first highlands member of the Pangu Pati (Party). Due to his experience in commercial activities and tree-cutting activities in his area, he is now the assistant minister for forests, and has recently been to Japan to negotiate a timber contract. Kundiawa and upper Chimbu are now represented by Father John Nilles, who has been in the district since 1937.

As New Guinea moves towards self-government, the Chimbus must increasingly understand and participate in national political movements. Their leaders must have not only the traditional abilities of orator and organizer, but an understanding of Papua New Guinea's political and economic goals.

Chapter 19

Plus ça change, plus c'est la même chose

CHIMBUS HAVE never felt that their way of life was stable and unchanging. All of their beliefs and traditions, their language, their social relations, their transactional society rest upon a fundamental premise that people constantly adapt and change with external conditions, interpersonal and intergroup relationships. There is no image of a fixed universe or social structure.

But this expectation of change was, before 1933, in a context of isolated tribal life and strife; it did not extend to the sudden introduction of utterly new things and people — the missions, the Australian administration, travelers and settlers from lowland Papua New Guinea and overseas, and the travel of Chimbus to other areas.

Insecurity and mistrust of strangers have not been fully eliminated by the presence of roads and government officials. In 1964, a road went through Gena tribe territory so we could drive in a large loop from Mintima through Kerowagi into Gena country and back in one afternoon. On such trips we often took Naregu tribesmen from Mintima and they were most anxious if we carried Gena tribesmen in the Land Rover. They urged us to put them down and said that they were afraid of sorcery from close contact. The older Mintima residents expressed awe and fear at such a journey.

The Chimbu interest in goods and the possession and circulation of valuable objects is also a key to their attitudes towards the white man's new things and ways. The evident technological superiority of metal, cloth and other western goods was sufficient proof of the superiority of the white man. For some time the spiritual concerns of the mission priest were not

121

seen as different from the administrative concerns of the *kiap*. Both had western objects which they might give Chimbus for services or trade for local produce. They did not have the same transactional relations as with other Chimbus, but there was a kind of exchange relationship. Mission teaching of Christian worship was restricted to church and mission school. Less evident in the early days was the political authority of the administration. The *kiap* in Kundiawa had an independent power center with a native police force. He was connected by road, radio and air to the central administration. The white man's empire was greater than any Chimbu could imagine. Soon other officials, visitors, settlers, shopkeepers and buyers of native produce appeared as evidence of the white man's huge world. Much later, Chimbu were employed and traveled to work in other areas and saw more of the world.

As time went on, the Chimbus began to discover what a low value their labor and produce had in exchange for the goods they wanted. When I first began work in the area, unskilled labor was worth only about $3.00 a month plus board and Chimbus sold food crops for a few cents a pound. But items like shirts, shovels, flashlights, enamel dishes, and tinned meat were all imported and sold at high prices in local shops.

I observed attitudes of Chimbus over a number of years. In 1958 they were beginning to sell coffee and use the money for purchasing goods in shops. They had a high expectation of rapid increase in standard of living. But they found that the slow hand-processing of coffee beans controlled their productivity, and thus the income they could expect. They saw that they could not accumulate the price of a car, a western style house, household goods, or a variety of clothing from their labor or the sale of their produce. Their income brought only an occasional single purchase of shorts, a knife, a padlock, or cooking pot.

In 1962, the inequality and distance between hope and reality became disturbingly evident. Widespread resentment against certain shopkeepers and coffee buyers was expressed. In a public meeting they were accused of cheating the people and an administration officer answered the accusation with a denial of dishonesty or discrimination. It was clear that the white man stood united against Chimbu. The Chimbu were helpless. There was no way they could improve their lot. Still no revolt was organized.

Their only successes came through gaining the ear and support of a government officer who would help them obtain a saw, a medical post, a coffee processing plant, etc. A successful leader was the man who had ideas about what he wanted to have for his group, and convinced an officer that they should be brought to his location. Such desires could be aired in the local government council and sometimes manipulated, so that the desired improvement came to the place of the particular councillor who started the drive.

The colonial situation establishes a particular kind of dependence. The people themselves have no direct means of obtaining the knowledge and capabilities which would allow them equal participation in a modern way of life. A non-literate community can only depend upon enlightened outside help for advancement. They cannot teach themselves. When they see other people living at a higher standard, they may desire those objects without any way of understanding how they have come to be. If they want these things, they inevitably feel helpless, and when they see the white man doing no hard physical labor, they are often unwilling to work for what is quite obviously to them very little material reward. Why should the *kiap* have his house built for him if the Chimbu must build his own house? The *kiap* only sits at a desk in the *hauspepa*. Yet they see the *kiap* in his *hauspepa* as having great power, and themselves as having none. It is the white man who brings in new crops and livestock, and provides the market for surplus production. Tools and machines are delivered to him, and he supplies all of the trained personnel, teachers, medical officers, agricultural officers, and judges. It was a very long time before any Chimbu were trained to do these jobs, and the Chimbus' knowledge of the cities, factories, universities, parliaments, manufacturing and administrative processes was only what they could pick up from those who visited or participated and told them about it. There were no Chimbu words in which to describe these things, and the Chimbu analogies of large buildings, large bodies of people, big groups coming together for discussion, could hardly portray the reality of urban western civilization.

I can remember the wonderment when, one day, Kondom (then member of the House of Assembly and president of the Local Government Council) told a group of people about his visit to Australia. In describing an elevator, he said, "We got into a little room. Then the door of the room closed by itself and after a little bit, the door opened again and we were in a different place." He told them how food was made in machines and eaten in restaurants. The land was cement, buildings were of brick. He built a stone house as an example.

To a Chimbu, the marvels of the gasoline engine are of the same character as the marvels of a trip to the moon. Woven wool or cotton is just as strange as woven man-made fiber. Seashells, glass beads and plastic bangles are equally exotic. This technological ignorance, nurtured by traditional stories of creation and the origin of things by ancestral heroes, is the basis of "cargo thinking" — the belief that the white man's ancestors are immensely powerful and concealing things from the black man. In Chimbu this has not taken the form of a "cargo cult" or messianic movement.

While western people and western influences are reaching, in different ways, to the whole of the Chimbu population, the youth of Chimbu is experiencing formal education of the type with which previous generations had no experience whatsoever. Some of them leave their homes and stay, for many months at a time, in a boarding school operated by either a mission or the government, and live under conditions of discipline and organization of an entirely new character. Other children go daily to school, leaving their huts in the morning and spending a number of hours in a schoolroom; their lessons follow a standard Australian curriculum.

The teachers are Europeans or New Guineans, but even those who are Chimbu are officially forbidden to use the Chimbu language as a medium of instruction. Instruction had been, until the 1960's, most commonly in Pidgin English, but this, too, is prohibited, and all instruction is to be in English. This means that, for the first year or two of school, while a child may have some acquaintance with Pidgin English, he has none with English as such, and whatever he learns comes to him through a language in which he has no previous familiarity. Both the language and the content of the lessons, then, are entirely new to him. Thus, while this takes place in his own community, it does so in a medium and with material of an entirely alien form.

This school material has little application to New Guinea life. Further, the ways of school mean nothing to adults. The standard American question, "And what did you do in school today?" is unimaginable. The only relevant content of the school day would be news of local people and their activities. If the teacher is a local person, his personal life or family activities might be of interest. But the schoolwork itself is too distant from anyone's experience to have any meaning in local life. A child who persists in school, going through the grades and acquiring real literacy and fluency in English, a genuine acquaintance with school subjects, such as literature, art, mathematics, history, geography, science and social science, either makes this an entirely separate mental realm, or himself becomes increasingly detached in his interests and thoughts from other people in the community. Chimbus feel the need of protection and support against more educated and sophisticated Papuans and New Guineans. To them, highlanders were "bush kanakas," backward and ignorant.

Thus, sources of information about western life, through schools or through individual representatives, presents a different social, political and economic system from that to which the people are accustomed. How, then, does social change take place? One might observe the adoption of elements of western culture; for example, the use of tools, clothing, technological activities, participation in government-sponsored councils, appearance at hospitals or at magistrate's courts, migration to work, the sale of cash crops and other produce, electing local government councillors and members of the House of Assembly, attending demonstrations by agricultural officers of new crops and processes — it would come to a very long

list of specific elements of behavior and activities which are introduced
from the Australian administration, its representaitves, or by individual
Chimbu who have visited outside and returned.

But there is not a split life for the Chimbu today. The Chimbu is both
a subsistence farmer and a coffee producer, at the same time. He allocates
his time, his week, his day, his efforts, interests and energies among the
various activities. Some are required, like attendance at government-
decreed activities, others are free personal choice between helping a friend
or a relative build a house or repair a fence, or taking his coffee to market.
The individual and collectively the group adopts these varied modes of
behavior, the knowledge about how to do certain tasks, the habit of ham-
mering nails or attending the medical-aid post for illnesses, or taking dispute cases to the *kiap* for settlement. This was especially evident in 1971
when numerous activities — garden preparation, pig feast dancing, as-
sembling to pay council tax, a wedding, and a performance of plays for
tourists — were all done by the Mintima people on one day.

The Chimbus do not classify or compartmentalize their behavior as new
or old or traditional or modern. They do not know that the sweet potato
entered from a South American source only a few hundred years ago. Of
course, many of the older people today can describe times before the white
man came, or the early days of colonial rule, and can remember the
course of changes which have taken place during their experience. But
these recollections are not always accurate, and it may not be of any importance to them that some ways of behaving are recent and others are
older.

One can, of course, see the cumulative effect of these introductions, and
I was able to observe some important phases of this transition; for
example, from traditional to manufactured clothing, and from cooking
in open fire or earth oven to the use of some imported foods and cooking in
pots. When such changes happen as rapidly as they have in Chimbu, they
have all of the elements of change in fashion, which we observe in modern
western communities. As the range of alternatives extends, some people
must be considered old-fashioned, while others are at the forefront of a new
trend. A fashion may suddenly drop out, or be replaced by a new one. New
forms and institutions of a more fundamental character also come in. The
medium of introduction is most frequently an individual or a government
officer, rather than, as in our society, popular media. But even this can
change when radios, television and widespread literacy come to a territory
like Chimbu. The result is a new kind of dynamic in life — wider horizons
and new sources of information, breaking the long-standing isolation of
Chimbu society. There are new sources for the new behavior; but the fact
of change of behavior is not different. The more things change, the more
they stay the same.

Appendix I

Glossary

Affines
> Relatives through marriage: a wife's close kinsman and the husband or wife of a sister or brother.

Agnates
> Kinsmen related patrilineally, as a line of descent through males: father to son, brothers, etc., including sisters and daughters but not their offspring.

Big Man (Chimbu: *yomba*-man, *pondo*-big)
> A leader in Melanesia; most New Guinea languages have such a term for a leader or important man.

Bosboi (Pidgin)
> Recognized native leader in early days of administration. Sometimes given a porcelain ring as a symbol of office, which was worn on a band, usually on the forehead. In some places given a hat.

Clan
> In Chimbu, an exogamous, patrilineal, named group, of several hundred members. Its land is in one or more blocks within the tribal territory.

Exogamy
> Prohibition of marriage within a group or to a category of relatives.

Hauspepa (Pidgin)
> The government office.

Kalabus (Pidgin)
> Jail or prison.

Kiap (Pidgin)
> An Australian officer of the Papua New Guinea administration.

Komdi (Pidgin)
> A member of a committee, most often a council committeeman.

Konsel (Pidgin)
> An elected councillor of a local government council.

128   Appendix I

Kot (Pidgin)
A "court" held by a local leader to discuss a dispute.
Laplap (Pidgin)
A hemmed length of cloth worn as a wrap-around skirt.
Lucky (Pidgin)
A card gambling game which resembles "21," widely played in Papua New Guinea.
Luluai (Pidgin)
An appointed New Guinea official responsible for a tribe, clan or village group. The term was adapted from Tolai of New Britain by the German administration. Given a hat or badge by the administration.
Matrilateral Kin
Kinsmen related through the mother, including her brothers and their children.
Non-agnate
A kinsman who is related by some other means than common agnatic descent. May include affines.
Patrilineal
Relationship or descent in the male line, as from father to son.
Pidgin English
A *lingua franca* in Melanesia whose vocabulary is mostly derived from English, with words from European, Melanesian and other languages. It is known as Neo-Melanesian because the grammar is close to Melanesian. Used between natives speaking different languages, and between Europeans and natives.
Prestation
A customary ceremonial gift which establishes or maintains a relationship between persons or groups.
Tambu (Pidgin)
Cowrie shell found off the coast in parts of Melanesia. The Tolai string tambu shell in lengths and it is a form of currency. In Chimbu it is sewn on cloth as a headband and exchanged at marriage. Also nassa shell.
Tribe
In Chimbu a named group with a territory, comprising several clans. May be composed of two distinct subtribes of different origin, *e.g.* Siambuga-Wauga.
Tultul (Pidgin)
An appointed New Guinea official in charge of a clan, subclan or village. The term was taken from Tolai by the German administration of New Guinea. Had a badge of office.

Appendix II

You and the Native

Notes for the Guidance of Members of the Forces in
their Relations with New Guinea Natives

Allied Geographical Section

Southwest Pacific Area

12th February 1943

G.H.Q., S.W.P.A.
12 February, 1943

Published for the information of all concerned.

By command of General MacARTHUR

R. K. SUTHERLAND
Major General, U.S.A.
Chief of Staff

OFFICIAL
B. M. FITCH,
Colonel, A.G.D.,
Adjutant General

OUR POTENTIAL ALLIES

1. The natives are a very important factor in the military situation. Their goodwill may decide whether we win or lose the Battle of New Guinea.
2. The natives are used to us, as white men; they feel we belong, whereas the Japanese are in every respect strangers. Natives don't like strangers. Therefore, their natural inclination is to side with us.
3. We are mighty lucky to start with this advantage. (It would certainly take a very long time to win without it). It is our business now to use the advantage properly and see that we keep it. Remember that with improper use it is always possible to lose it.
4. Another reason why the native sides with us is that he prefers our manners to those of the enemy. We shall have therefore to remember our manners, never descending to the level of the Japanese.
5. Remember that the natives are our real or potential allies. Keep on the right side of them.

THE NATIVE AS A HUMAN BEING

6. The native is nearly, if not quite, as good a man as you are. Don't underrate his intelligence. The big difference is that you and your forefathers have had better opportunities.
7. At any rate he plays a good game on his home ground. He shows up better than you do in the tropical forest or the sago-swamp. In New Guinea bushcraft, in hardihood, in mobility, he leaves you standing.
8. Don't believe it when you are told he has the mentality of a child. That is rubbish. An adult native is an adult. He has a grown-up mind, grown-up feelings, and grown-up dignity. Respect them all.
9. A great authority (Sir Hubert Murray, Governor of Papua for more than 30 years) reached the conclusion that natives were mostly "gentlemen," meaning that they had regard for other people's feelings. It is up to us to play the gentleman also.
10. At any rate the native is an ordinary human being. You have to treat him with the proper amount of tact if you want to get good service out of him.

THE ATTITUDE OF SUPERIORITY

11. The native has always looked up to the white man.
He admires him because of the marvellous things
that white men at large can do——make electric torches,
fly in aeroplanes, etc. You may not be marvellous yourself, but he will think you are, merely because you are
one of the white race.

12. He is also rather afraid of the white men, with all
the power of their civilisation behind them. Therefore he is rather afraid of you.

13. It is not too much to say that he stands in awe of
us. He thinks we are superior beings. We may not
all deserve this reputation, but it is worth acting
up to.

14. Always therefore maintain your position or pose of
superiority, even if you sometimes have doubts
about it. It is flattering to the vanity and in the
circumstances must pay us well. As for the native, he
will not resent it, because he has brought it about
himself and he is used to it.

CONDUCT TOWARDS NATIVES IN GENERAL

15. Do not, however, ride the high horse over him. Act
rather as if you were his superior, but only
slightly his superior.

16. Don't bully him. It would be too easy. You are 11
or 12 stone to his 8; you can use your fists and he
knows nothing of that; and you have a rifle and bayonet
of which he is naturally much afraid. It would, therefore, be, to say the least, unsporting.

17. Another reason why you should not bully him is that
he will not like it, and therefore you will not get
the best service out of him.

18. Don't curse and swear at him either. He detests
that, and it is not a fair go, for if he dares to
answer you back you will call it insolence, and proceed
to stronger measures. Remember that it is insolence to
swear at a man in the first place.

19. And don't make fun of him unless he is at least
partly in the joke.

20. Joke with him by all means; even lark with him. He

likes it as much as you do. But while you play the
fool don't forget that you have to maintain that pose
of superiority. Don't go too far.
21. Don't deliberately descend to his level. He has
    not been used to that from the white man; he will
consider it unfitting and think less of you.
22. Don't clasp him round the neck. Brotherhood is all
    right. But don't act like a twin brother. Be very
much the big brother.
23. Always, without overdoing it, be the master. The
    time may come when you will want a native to obey
you. He won't obey you if you have been in the habit of
treating him as an equal.

CONDUCT IN VILLAGES

24. Don't enter a village as if it entirely belonged
    to you. It belongs to the natives. But enter it with
some show of confidence, as if you expected a friendly
welcome. In any settled district you are likely to get
it, because that is the natives' habit.
25. Needless to say, you have to deserve it by good be-
    haviour. If you behave badly the natives will prob-
ably clear out and leave you on your uppers. And when
you come to the next village, and the next, you may find
them empty. Bad behaviour on the part of one or two men
can ruin the prospects of your whole party.
26. Do not butt in on village affairs. If a feast or
    ceremony is going forward you may do well to show
an interest, but only as a bystander. Don't go so far
as to hold things up by your questions. You will then
have become a nuisance. If you think the native carry-
ings-on are laughable, don't laugh.
27. If you see queer things stuck up on village houses,
    on the verandahs, or in the village square, leave
them alone. They may be sacred or magical signs. Don't
beat a drum without first asking if you may. As often
as not the village drums are under tabu. If you see a
twist of leaves tied round the butt of a coconut palm
or a fruiting tree, it is a tabu mark. It is meant to
stay there. Try another tree.

PAYMENT

28. In districts under our control the natives have

been instructed to help and have been promised rewards for doing so. They can give you food, shelter and
information, and they can guide you on your way. Express your thanks. Pay if you can.

29. Pay is important. The native economic system is
     one of reciprocity, which just means, "tit for tat."
Give him something for services rendered, even if is
only half a stick of tobacco, a fish-hook or a razor-
blade.

30. Do not overpay. For one thing the uneducated native
     has no idea of money values and may make ridiculous
demands. For another thing, shrewd eggs will be out for
what they can get. (They have been heard to demand 2/-
for a single coconut and a case of meat for a bunch of
bananas). Learn the current prices and do not exceed
them.

31. Here is a rough scale of pre-war prices. They refer
     to villages. In towns (or encampments), you may
have to pay twice as much. It is only a general guide,
not a fixed scale: prices vary according as the food in
question is plentiful or not. Values may be changing in
wartime; if in doubt consult ANGAU.

> (Prices are given in tobacco,
> 3 sticks = 1/- to the native).

Coconuts	
5-10 (according to district)	For 1 stick
Bananas	
Small bunch	" 1 "
Bananas	
Big Bunch	Up to 3 sticks
Pineapples	
1-3 (according to size)	For 1 stick
Oranges	
12	" 1 "
Pawpaws	
3 or 4 (say 12 lbs.)	" 1 "
Taro	
Small basketful (say 12 lbs.)	" 1 "
Sweet Potatoes	
Small basketful (say 12 lbs.)	" 1 "
Yams	
Small basketful (say 12 lbs.)	" 1 "

Sago
   Bundle of about 25 lbs.   "   1½   "
   (Rate, ¼d. per lb.)
32. Good trade lines, easy for the individual to carry,
       are beads, matches, razor-blades, handkerchiefs,
fish-hooks, fish-lines, red and black "paint" powder.
Even a needle with a yard or so of thread is acceptable.
       Larger lines are hatchets, knives, pocket knives,
files, mirrors, calico, belts, pouches, mouth organs,
etc.
       Coarse salt goes well in the mountains. A dessert-
spoonful is worth a stick of tobacco.
33. Conserve your tobacco supply. If you want to give
       the native a tip, don't think you have to give him
a whole stick; give him half an inch. Keep your old
newspapers for the natives' cigarettes.
34. If you have nothing, give him at least a chit, or
       "paper," for receipt. See that you write decently,
giving your name, his name, the date and the circumstances. He will be able to cash in on it later on.
35. Never allow begging. Native children soon get the
       habit if encouraged. Don't make unnecessary pres-
ents of tins of meat to anyone. Remember the tit for tat
principle. Anyway, there is not so much food in New
Guinea that you can afford to give it way for nothing.

THREE GOLDEN RULES

36. Remember three things in any village—gardens, pigs
       and women. They are of basic importance in the lives
of New Guinea natives, and interference with any of
them will bring trouble to you and your mates. Don't
forget this. Stick it in your hat.
GARDENS:—
37. Natives depend on their own small gardens in which
       they grow enough to support themselves only, with
some surplus for an occasional feast. A large body of
troops would eat them out in no time. You cannot expect
them to go hungry on your account.
38. If there are no natives about and you have to help
       yourselves to food in a garden, leave some payment.
Tie some tobacco to a stick and stick it in the ground
near where you pulled the taro or cut the sugar-cane.

Leave your "mark" also on a piece of paper—your name,
and a picture of the Union Jack or the Stars and Stripes.
Tie it round the gift. The native does this sort of
thing himself and he will understand.

VILLAGE PIGS:-

39. Be most careful about village pigs. They are not
   always on sale like meat in a butcher's stall. The
native values them very highly, fattening them for some
special occasion. He may not wish to sell at all, and
anyway the price is high. (In remoter parts you might
get one for an axe, but the price may be £5 on the coast.)
If you see a pig within a mile of a village, then ten to
one it is a village pig, not a wild one. You will probably find it has a slit in its ear. Don't shoot at sight.
Bargain first. Hardly anything can upset the natives
more than taking his pigs.

NATIVE WOMEN:-

40. There's only one thing to be more careful about
   than village pigs, and that is village women.
41. Among some tribes the women associate readily with
   Europeans; in others they will not associate at all.
Even where they do there are two parties to consider:
(1) the women themselves, (2) their menfolk.
42. If the woman is not consenting, then intercourse is
   just rape—whether the victim be white or brown.
Under the laws of New Guinea it is a hanging matter.
43. If the men (husbands, fathers or brothers) are not
   consenting, then it is at least a very serious kind
of interference. If they do not seek their revenge,
they will at least clear out, taking their women with
them, and you will lose their co-operation.
44. In any case, an affair with a native woman is not a
   love-match; it is a deal. You are expected to pay.
45. The personal risks are granuloma, gonnorrhoea, and
   (where the Japanese have got there first) syphilis.

NATIVE OFFICIALS

46. On entering a village make a bee-line for the native officials, if there are any. They are paid by
the Administration and wear uniforms or badges. They
have some authority over the villagers, and it is their
duty to help white men. (If they greet you with a rather

unusual kind of salute, return it and keep a straight face).

47. The village officials are:—

Papua: Village Constable (V.C.). Always called the "Village Policeman." Blue serge jumper and loin cloth and red sash.

Village Councillor: "Medal" only.

Mandated Territory of New Guinea: Paramount Luluai (for large districts, 30-50 villages). Cap, broad red band, white cap cover, staff. Luluai—cap, broad red band. Tultul—cap, two narrow red bands. Medical Tultul —cap, white band, red cross.

The uniform may be much tattered, like your own. But the native has a high respect for it; make it appear that you do also.

48. Appeal in the first place to the Village Policeman or the Luluai (or Paramount Luluai if you happen to meet him). If he is not in the village when you arrive, ask for him; he will probably come at the double. He has to keep up a position in front of the villages, so don't let him down by disrespectful treatment. Kid to him a little. He will arrange for food, if there is any to be had; also for shelter and carriers.

IMPORTANT VILLAGERS

49. Only one village in half-a-dozen will have a Village Policeman or a Luluai. But every village has a leader or headman, usually a middle-aged man. He is the village spokesman and has some real authority. He may not be easy to distinguish, for there are, generally speaking, no big chiefs in New Guinea and no marks of chieftainship. But you should be able to pick him. Having done so, treat him well, using a touch of ceremony.

50. New Guinea natives pay great respect to age. Therefore go out of your way to address the old men. Give them a smoke. They are still very important. The whole village will appreciate this attention.

51. Some young men, "Smart Alecs," may press forward. They are not likely to be of real importance in the village. But do not snub them or brush them aside too readily. They are progressives, and may be very useful.

MISSION BOYS

52. Do not be swayed by idle talk against the Missions.
Their presence in New Guinea has made your way much easier. You can thank them, incidentally, for the fact that many natives can understand your English. Never jeer at a Mission boy simply because he is a Mission boy.

53. Mission teachers are likely to be specially useful.
They have more influence over the natives than does the Village Constable or the Luluai. They will also understand your needs better. They have a fine tradition of hospitality towards white men.

54. In the (former) Mandated Territory some Mission teachers (Lutheran and Catholic) are suspected of having German sympathies. But even so you should be able to depend on them to help you against the Japanese.

COMMUNICATING IDEAS

55. There may be a great deal of jabbering and shouting in the village when you first arrive. Keep cool and be patient; it will simmer down. Don't join in, but find a man who can talk some English, take him aside and tell him clearly, quietly and slowly what you want.

56. Use the simplest words you can. If he cannot understand, remember that raising your voice won't help. And don't get angry. It's not his responsibility to know your language.

57. Make every effort, now, to learn Police-Motu for use in Papua; Pidgin-English for use in the Mandated Territory. If it doesn't get you an extra stripe, it may one day get you a feed. On the side you will get some fun out of learning these comic languages.

58. Remember that the language difficulty lies at the root of misunderstanding and friction. Don't think a native stupid because he can't understand your foreign tongue; if anyone is stupid it is you for not knowing his. Don't think him silly, or mischievous, or a liar because he says he understands what you want and then does something entirely different. The fact is probably that you did not get your meaning across.

59. The native is anxious to please. He, too, often gives you the answer he thinks you want rather than the true answer. Therefore be careful not to sug-

gest an answer when you put a question. If you show annoyance when he says "Yes" and then, to make sure, put the question again, he will as like as not say "No."

60. He is rather a ready liar in any case, for he has not been brought up like George Washington to think that lying is a very serious matter. Don't swallow the first man's story whole. Try out some other informants (independently, not in a group; a group of natives usually speaks as one man).

61. Even when he thinks he is telling the truth the native is a great exaggerator—whether about the number of dead or the size of mountains. Take it with a grain of salt. Be critical.

62. One small point is worth noting. Don't put questions in the "negative" form. Let us suppose there are no Japanese in the native's village. You say to him, "Are there any Japanese in your village?" He answers, truthfully, "No." If you say to him, "There are no Japanese in your village, are there?" He will answer, "Yes." He is still speaking the truth. He means, "Yes, there are not." In short the word for "Yes" in nearly all languages but our own means simply, "I agree with you." Remember this point if you don't want to be misled.

63. You can always fall back on sign-language. One or two points are as follows:—

The commonest way of counting is by doubling the fingers into the palm of the hand, starting with the little finger. Clench your fist for 5; clench both fists and hold them together for 10.

To extend the left arm and flick the fingers near the right ear means shooting an arrow or firing a rifle. It will be used as a sign to indicate the presence of the enemy.

To place the palm of the hand on the cheek and bend the head sideways indicates a "sleep" or a day's stage on a journey.

Beckon with the palm of your hand down, not up.

Don't point. Natives don't seem to get it. If you want to indicate something near at hand the best way is to go and touch it.

You can easily invent signs to show that you want food or drink.

HOSTILE NATIVES

64. "Generally speaking," to quote an experienced New
    Guinea prospector, "natives civilised and uncivilised are friendly and therefore should be treated as friends, not as black bastards who intend to murder you at the slightest chance." There are hardly any "wild" natives left in New Guinea; certainly none in the well-known parts where troops are operating.

65. Reasons for possible hostility are—(1) Fear of the
    complete stranger; (2) co-operation with the enemy;
(3) vengeance for ill-treatment.

    But (1) you, being a white man, are not a complete stranger. Natives have been used to the likes of you for 50 years. (2) Generally speaking, the natives prefer to co-operate with us, not with the enemy. (3) If you and your mates always give the natives a good spin they will have nothing to avenge.

66. If therefore you ever find yourself lost in the
    bush, don't be afraid of the native population.
Make it your first object to find some of them. They represent your best, perhaps your only, chance of survival.

67. The only time or place in which you need fear making contact with the natives is when you are near
the enemy. They may be working with him and they may have been promised rewards for capturing you. The obvious thing then is to sneak off. When you think you are at a safe distance, find some natives and take your chance. It should be a good one.

68. If you see a spear stuck in the middle of the path
    and pointing towards you, or if you see some twisted
grass on a strip of bark stretched across the track, it is a sign that the natives do not want you to proceed. It may mean they are hostile.

69. Bide your time. Shout. If they are anywhere near
    they will soon come and have you under observation.
And if you are alone they are not likely to hurt you, because they will not be much afraid of one man. If there are a number of you, they won't hurt you either, because then they will be afraid.

70. If you have a friendly native with you as a guide,

get him to do the shouting. That is the native fashion. He will announce your harmlessness and your good
intentions. (If you think the enemy are near, it is of
course a different matter. It may be the wrong thing to
shout then, but that is because of the enemy, and we are
talking about natives.)

71. If no one comes in answer to your shouting, it prob-
     ably means there is no one within earshot. Proceed,
keeping your eyes open. You've got to take your chance
anyway. The alternative is possibly to starve.

72. When you reach the village enter it confidently as
     you do a gate with "Beware of the Dog" on it. Don't
show fear, and don't start brandishing your walking
stick, or the dog may try to bite you. It will certainly
snarl if only under its breath.

73. Natives will soon dribble in if they are not there
     already. They will be curious and probably rather
frightened (i.e., if they are at all "wild") and only
too anxious to make up to you. Have a smoke ; give them a
smoke ; ask for some food ; pay for it if you can.

74. If the women remain in a village on your entry, all
     is well ; the native "trusts" you. If they clear at
the first sign of your approach, it means that he is
suspicious. It is wise then to be on your guard. But
when the women start to trickle back, you have the "all
clear" signal for certain.

75. When in a strange village keep a good lookout on
     your stores and property. Natives are skilful
thieves. If you are sure something has been stolen
you've got to make a row about it. Get it back or exact
some fair penalty.

76. If the natives actually oppose you, throwing spears
     and shooting arrows, fire a shot over their heads.
This has been the Government method in New Guinea for
60 years. It nearly always acts. Only in the last ex-
tremity might a Government officer shoot to kill, and
then he had to explain his way through a court of inquiry. You are now getting the benefit of 60 years of
humane and sensible pacification. Try to keep up the
standard.

77. Bear in mind that native bowmen can't shoot straight
     at any decent range and a man can't throw a spear

any distance. Dodging bullets is unfortunately not possible; but dodging spears and arrows is a recognised
part of native warfare.

78. If you have natives (police or others) under your
     control, keep a strict hand over them when in
strange country. If they thieve or play up with women,
the natives will naturally turn hostile or clear out.
It is your responsibility.

79. If you have had a clash with hostile natives and
     have had maybe to kill one or two of them, don't
follow it up with a general revenge. Don't go in for
"shooting up," and don't set fire to houses. The natives will have had enough, and it will pay you best to
make friends again as soon as you can.

80. But the main thing, to repeat, is that the natives
     are very unlikely to attack you. Don't expect it.

LABOUR

81. You may some day find yourself in charge of a gang
     of labourers or a line of carriers. If you have
some power of command and a good temper, and if you have
remembered that air of superiority, you will get good
work out of them. If not, hand over to someone else.

82. Be both considerate and firm. In the words of a
     miner, "You must be boss, father and mother to them
all."

83. Pay full attention to their food, shelter, cloth-
     ing, health, tobacco and pay.

84. Natives are not always good at keeping their own
     promises. But old-timers agree that if _you_ make a
promise to a native you must keep it. So make none that
you don't intend to keep or can't keep.

85. You must be judge in their disputes. None are too
     trivial for your notice. Do your best to get to the
bottom of them. Have no favourites and don't get anyone
set.

86. Leave slave-driving to the Japanese. Your men
     should have reasonable hours and a right to their
leisure. Alternatively you may give them reasonable
daily "tasks" which they can finish in their own time.

87. The native does not expect the white man to do
     manual labour. He is ready to do the hard work or

the dirty work himself under the white man's supervision. But remember what you expect from your own officers and N.C.O.'s.—that one who gives an order should be ready, if need be, to carry it out himself. Do not demand the impossible, whether in working hours or weight of loads.

88. At the same time they like the white boss who is a worker and a cheerful one. And they will respond to example. If you can sing, sing. They will be tickled to death.

89. All orders should be given in an even manner and as though you expect they will be obeyed. Let no shade of doubt enter into your voice.

90. Don't stand any nonsense. You are bound to find some loafers, pointers and malingerers. Watch them and keep them up to it. Be firm from the start. Don't let them put it over you. For malingerers, try the thermometer.

91. There may be a bad egg who deliberately defies you, just to try you out. There is only one thing to do in these circumstances. Crack him.

92. But always try to keep your temper. If there is anything the native hates it is a bad tempered boss. Don't abuse him and don't nag. If you find yourself specially irritated by the way your labourers are behaving, take some more quinine and a dose of salts.

93. Try not to mess them about. Get a clear idea of what you want and tell or show them clearly what it is. Be as patient as you can when they get hold of the wrong end of the stick. It's mostly your fault anyway.

94. The native knows very little about your way of life. If you are very lucky enough to get a personal servant or a cook remember that you have to teach him his business. Try to be amused rather than angry if he mixes the sardines with the jam.

95. Don't lay about you. Punching natives grows into a habit with some people. They even boast of their victories. But it is a bad habit; for one thing the victories are too easy; and for another the practice pays badly in the long run. Old-timers will tell you that, and they <u>know.</u>

96. The native puts up with a lot. But if a man treats

his labourers too badly they will desert, and when
they have fled into the New Guinea bush he will not get
them back in a hurry.

97. In the natives' code of morals revenge is a good
    deed. The man who habitually ill-treats his labour-
ers is the sort of man they would betray to the Japanese if they got a chance. And who shall say that he
would not deserve it?

98. But New Guinea revenge is not always fixed on the
    guilty individual. It commonly falls on one of his
kinsmen or fellow tribesman. So, if one of your cobbers
ill-treats a labourer, you may be the man to die for it.

TO SUM UP

99. The natives have a big opinion of Europeans in gen-
    eral, but they will test you and size you up as an
individual. Your conduct can raise or lower the general
standard. You are therefore a guardian of the white
man's prestige. It is a very important obligation.

100. Remember finally that the New Guinea natives are
     one of the world's Backward Peoples, and that Aus-
tralia undertook to regard their welfare as a "sacred
trust." They are now in an unfortunate position. This
fight is not theirs, and they might well be excused for
wanting to keep out of it. But at the same time we absolutely need their help in order to win. So we may have
to make them work for us whether they like it or not.
That is a hard thing. But it will come easier to them,
and the work will be better, if we try to deserve our
prestige and treat them fair.

References

Aufenanger, H.
1959 The War-Magic Houses in the Wahgi Valley and Adjacent Areas. *Anthropos* 54: 1-26.
1960 The Kanggi Spirit in the Central Highlands of New Guinea. *Anthropos* 55, 5-6: 671-688.

Barrau, J.
1965 Witnesses of the Past: Notes on Some Food Plants of Oceania. *Ethnology* IV: 282-294.

Blackwood, B.
1950 The Technology of a Modern Stone Age People in New Guinea. *Pitt-Rivers Museum Occasional Papers on Technology.* Oxford.

Boserup, E.
1965 *The Conditions of Agricultural Growth.* Chicago: Aldine Publ. Co.

Bowers, N.
1971 Demographic Problems in Montane New Guinea. In S. Polgar (ed.) *Culture and Population: A Collection of Current Studies.* Carolina Population Center Monograph No. 9, Chapel Hill.

Brandewie, E.
1971 The Place of the Big Man in Traditional Hagen Society in the Central Highlands of New Guinea. *Ethnology* 11: 194-210.

Brookfield, H. C.
1964 The Ecology of Highland Settlement. In *Am. Anthrop. Special Publ.: New Guinea, the Central Highlands,* ed. J. Watson, Vol. 66, No. 4, part 2: 20-38.
1968 The Money that Grows on Trees. *Australian Geographical Studies* 6: 97-119.
1971 *Melanesia.* London: Methuen.

Brookfield, H. C. and Brown, P.
1963 *Struggle for Land: Agriculture and Group Territories among the Chimbu of the New Guinea Highlands.* Melbourne: Oxford Univ. Press.

Brookfield, H. C. and White, J. P.
1968 Revolution or Evolution in the Prehistory of the New Guinea Highlands: A Seminar Report. *Ethnology* 7: 43-52.

Brown, P.
1960 Chimbu Tribes: Political Organization in the Eastern Highlands of New Guinea. *Southwestern J. Anthrop.* 16: 22-35.
1961 Chimbu Death Payments. *J. Roy. Anthrop. Inst.* 91: 77-96.
1962 Non-agnates among the Patrilineal Chimbu. *J. Polynesian Soc.* 71: 57-64.
1963 From Anarchy to Satrapy. *Am. Anthrop.* 65: 1-15.
1964 Enemies and Affines. *Ethnology* 3: 335-356.

145

1967a The Chimbu Political System. *Anthropological Forum* 2: 36-52.
1967b Kondom. *Journal of the Papua and New Guinea Society*, 1, 2: 3-11.
1969 Marriage in Chimbu. In *Pigs, Pearlshells and Women*, eds. R. M. Glasse and M. J. Meggitt, pp. 77-95. Englewood Cliffs, N.J.: Prentice Hall.
1970a Chimbu Transactions. *Man* 5: 99-117.
1970b Mingge-Money: Economic Change in the New Guinea Highlands. *Southwestern J. Anthrop.* 26: 242-260.

Brown, P. and Brookfield, H. C.
1967 Chimbu Settlement and Residence: A Study of Patterns, Trends and Idiosyncracy. *Pacific Viewpoint* 8: 119-151.

Brown, P. and Winefield, G.
1965 Some Demographic Measures Applied to Chimbu Census and Field Data. *Oceania* XXXV: 175-190.

Bulmer, R. N. H.
1960 Leadership and Social Structure among the Kyaka People of the Western Highlands District of New Guinea. Ph.D. dissertation, Australian National University.

Burridge, K. O. L.
1960 *Mambu*. London: Methuen.

Chagnon, N.
1968 *Yanomamo, the Fierce People*, New York: Holt-Rinehart-Winston.

Criper, C.
1967 The Politics of Exchange: A Study of Ceremonial Exchange amongst the Chimbu. Thesis, Australian National University.

Eastern Highlands Councillor
1960 Vol. I. Mimeographed in Goroka, New Guinea.

Epstein, A. L.
1969 *Matupit*. Canberra: Australian National University Press.

Epstein, T. S.
1968 *Capitalism, Primitive and Modern*. Canberra: Autralian National University Press.

Fel, E. and Hofer, T.
1969 *Proper Peasants*. Viking Fund Publications in Anthropology 46.

Finney, B. R.
1969 *New Guinean Entrepreneurs*. New Guinea Research Unit Bulletin 27.

Gardner, R. and Heider, K.
1968 *Gardens of War*. Random House: New York.

Glasse, R. M.
1968 *Huli of Papua*. Paris: Mouton.

Hanson, F. A.
1970 *Rapan Lifeways*. Boston: Little, Brown.

Hide, R. L.
1971 Land Demarcation and Disputes in the Chimbu District of the New Guinea Highlands. In *Land Tenure and Economic Development: Problems and Policies in Papua-New Guinea and Kenya*. New Guinea Research Unit Bulletin 40.

Kambkama
n.d. My Kuman Forebears ms.

Leahy, M. and Crain, M.
1937 *The Land that Time Forgot*. New York: Funk & Wagnalls.
Lowman-Vayda, C.
1968 Maring Big Men. *Anthropological Forum* 11: 180-198.
Mair, L. P.
1948 *Australia in New Guinea*. London: Christophers.
Malinowski, B.
1926 *Crime and Custom in Savage Society*. London: Kegan Paul.
Meggitt, M. J.
1958 The Enga of the New Guinea Highlands. *Oceania* 28: 253-330.
Nilles, P. J.
1940 Eine Knaben-Jugendweihe bei den Ostlichen Waugla im Bismarckge-birge Neugineas. *Int. Arch. für Ethnographie* 38: 93-98.
1943/4 Natives of the Bismarck Mountains, New Guinea. *Oceania* 14: 104-24; 15: 1-19.
1942/5 Digging-sticks, Spades, Hoes, Axes and Adzes of the Kuman People in the Bismarck Mountains of East-Central New Guinea. *Anthropos* 37-40: 205-212.
1950 The Kuman of the Chimbu Region, Central Highlands, New Guinea. *Oceania* 21: 25-65.
1953 The Kuman People: A Study of Cultural Change in a Primitive Society in the Central Highlands of New Guinea. *Oceania* 24: 1-27, 119-131.
Powell, J. M.
1970 The History of Agriculture in the New Guinea Highlands. *Search* 1: 199-200.
Read, K. E.
1959 Leadership and Consensus in a New Guinea Society. *Am. Anthrop.* 61: 425-436.
Reay, M.
1959 *The Kuma: Freedom and Conformity in the New Guinea Highlands*. Melbourne: Melbourne Univ. Press.
1964 Present-day Politics in the New Guinea Highlands. In *Am. Anthrop. Special Publ: New Guinea, the Central Highlands*. Ed. J. Watson, 66, 4, part 2: 340-356.
Robbins, R. G.
1963 Correlations of Plant Patterns and Population Migration into the Australian New Guinea Highlands. In J. Barrau (ed.) *Plants and the Migrations of Pacific People*: 45-59. Honolulu.
Salisbury, R. F.
1962 *From Stone to Steel: Economic Consequences of Technological Change in New Guinea*. Melbourne.
1964 Despotism and Australian Administration in the New Guinea High-lands. In *Am. Anthrop. Special Publ.: New Guinea, the Central High-lands*. ed. J. Watson, 66, 4, part 2: 225-239.
Schaefer, A.
1938 Zur Initiation im Wagi-tal. *Anthropos* 33: 401-423.
1938 'Kavagl' der Mann mit der Zaunpfahlkeule: Ein Beitrag zur Individuen-forschung. *Anthropos* v 33: 107-113.
1942 Ein Frauenbegrabnis bei den Korugu im Wagi-Tal. *Ethnos* 7: 25-43.
1945 Haus und Siedlung in Zentral-Neuguinea. *Ethnos* 10: 97-114.

148

Stanner, W. E. H.
  1956   The Dreaming. In *Australian Signpost*. Ed. T. A. G. Hungerford, Melbourne: F. W. Cheshire: 51-65.
Strathern, A. J.
  1966   Despots and Directors in the New Guinea Highlands. *Man* 1: 356-367.
  1971   Cargo and Inflation in Mount Hagen. *Oceania* 41: 255-65.
Vial, L. G.
  1942   They Fight for Fun. *Walkabout* 9: i, 5-9.
Watson, J. B.
  1965   From Hunting to Horticulture in the New Guinea Highlands. *Ethnology* 4: 295-309.
Willis, I.
  1969   Who Was First? The First White Man into the New Guinea Highlands. *Journal of the Papua and New Guinea Society*. 4, 1, 32-45.
Wurm, S. A.
  1961   The Languages of the Eastern, Western and Southern Highlands, Territory of Papua and New Guinea. In *Linguistic Survey of the South-Western Pacific,* ed. A. Capell. Revised ed. Noumea.

Index

Adolescence, 31-32, 41, 45, 48, 52
Adoption, 31, 52, 53, 61, 63
Agriculture: crops, 16, 21, 66, 88; *See also* Coffee; Pandanus Tree; Sweet Potatoes; Taro; history of, in Chimbu, 9-10, 15-21; techniques for, 11, 16, 18, 19, 19-20, 79
Aufenanger, H., 27

Barnes, J. A., xii-ix, 2
Barrau, J., 17
Birth, 30, 50
Blackwood, B., 16
Boserup, E., 17
Bowers, N., 18
Brandewie, E., 43
Brookfield, H. C., 2, 10, 12, 16, 83, 89, 92
Bulmer, R. N. H., 60
Burridge, K. O. L., 79

"Cargo" thinking, 8, 79, 123
Casuarina trees, 18-19, 59, 71
Ceremonies. *See* Feasts
Chagnon, N., 16
Childhood, 30-31, 52
"Chimbu", meaning of, 24
Clan, 35-37, 40, 43, 46, 48
Climate, 10 19, 51-52. *See also* Agriculture
Clothing, 7, 50, 79, 82, 83-84
Coffee, 27-28, 48, 71, 73, 76, 89-92
Colonial administration: functions of, 25-28, 57, 69-73; relationship of, to natives, 67, 98, 99, 115, 116. *See also* Government.
Conflict. *See* Fighting
Cosmological beliefs. *See* Religion
Courts, 103, 104, 106-109

Criper, C., 7
Crops. *See* Agriculture; Coffee; Pandanus trees; Sweet potatoes; Taro

Dancing, 47, 48-49
Dani, 60
Death, 53, 61
Death payments, 49, 50, 54, 114

Eastern highlands, 20, 23, 47, 60, 99
Ecology. *See* Agriculture; Climate
Economy: business, native, 27-28, 83, 89, 92; economic change, 27-28, 82, 85, 86-92, 95-96, 122; economic system, pre-colonial, 15, 45-46, 47, 49, 54, 86; trade, pre-colonial, 14, 16, 26, 40, 79, 86
Education, 65, 87, 94, 98, 110; schools, 27, 70, 74-75, 114, 124
Enga, 60
Epstein, A. L., 6
Epstein, T. S., 6, 91
Exogamy, 36, 38, 42, 50

Family life, 29-35. *See also* Marriage; Sexual behavior; Sex roles; Women
Feasts, 11, 37, 40, 54, 57, 93; continuance of, under colonial administration, 75-76, 84, 97, 112, 119; pig feast, 43, 47-50, 53; vegetable feast, 45, 46-47
Fighting (conflict), 7, 19, 39, 43, 51-67, 101-109; murder, 55-56, 60, 109; pacification by colonial administration, 25-26, 57, 65-67, 71-72, 110
Finney, B. R., 89
Firth, R., 12
Folklore, 5, 61, 63

Food 15, 46, 51, 84. *See also* Agriculture; Pandanus trees; Pigs; Sweet potatoes; Taro

Gardner, R., and Heider, K., 60
Glasse, R. M., 21
Government, native: pre-colonial, 51, 52, 55, 64; under colonial administration, 28, 73, 95-100, 112-113, 115-119. *See also* Colonial administration; Leaders, native

Hide, R. L, 109
History of Chimbu, 14-22
Household, 32-34, 45-46
Houses, 10, 17, 34, 48, 79; newer types, 82, 84, 89

Inheritance, 32, 44, 93, 101
Initiation, 48. *See* Adolescence

Kambkama, 59
Kinship, 32, 35-40, 50, 52, 53, 63
Kondom, 2, 68, 92, 110-20

Land, 19, 51-52, 62, 63; acquisition, 30, 32, 41, 54
Language: Chimbu 6, 12, 14; Pidgin, 76, 99
Law, 103-109, 112, 116. *See also* Punishment
Leaders, native: pre-colonial, 39, 41, 42-44, 53, 93; under colonial administration, 26, 43, 70-73, 89, 92, 93-100, 110-120
Leahy, M., 4, 9, 23-24, 65, 66, 78-79
Lowman-Vayda, C. 43

Magic. *See* Ritual; Sorcery
Mair, L. P., 8
Malinowski, B., 55
Marriage, 3-32, 33, 38, 45, 49-50, 75; courting, 31; divorce, 52; marriage payments, 39, 54, 58, 85, 91, 116; polygamy, 32, 33, 45, 75, 101
Medicine, 20, 73-74, 75, 93

Meggitt, M. J., 60
Migration, 20-21, 39, 40, 60-63, 70, 106
Missions, 8, 25, 27, 74-76
Money. *See* Economy; Economic change
Music, 48, 49
Mythology, *See* Religion

Nadel, S. F., 2
Nilles, J., 2, 27, 67, 81, 120

Occupations, 26-27, 67, 70-71, 74, 76, 86-88
Old age, 6-7, 19, 33, 44, 93

Pandanus trees, 30, 46, 47
Pigs, 17, 29, 63-64, 103-105
Population density, 10, 16, 18, 20-21, 26, 52
Population redistribution. *See* Migration
Powell, J., 15
Pre-history, 9, 10, 14-22
Prestige, 41-44, 47-48, 50, 64, 88, 93
Property, 44, 55-56, 101
Punishment, 51, 99, 102, 105, 108, 109. *See also* Law

Read, K. E., 43
Reay, M., 19, 43
Religion, 5-6, 7, 49, 52-53, 56, 59, 64. *See also* Missions
Ritual, 49, 52, 93
Robbins, R. G., 20

Salisbury, R. F., 43, 88
Schaefer, A., 2, 27, 74, 110
Settlement pattern, 16-18, 29, 32-33, 38-39
Sexual behavior, 30, 32, 55, 109
Sex roles, 7, 30, 76. *See also* Women
Shelter. *See* Houses
Social change: in Chimbu, 69-77, 88-89, 98-99, 101-102, 121-125; general theory of, 3, 5, 6, 9-13; native attitude towards, 5-8, 65-68, 116

Social structure, 9, 21, 29-40, 42-43, 53-56, 77, 86; cooperation, 32, 34-35, 46, 53-55, 95. *See also* Kinship; Prestige

Sorcery, 53, 66-67, 75-76, 109, 121

Spirits, 20, 48-49, 53

Stanner, W. E. H., 2, 6

Strathern, A. J., 43, 79

Subclan, 31, 35-37

Sweet potatoes, 9, 11, 16, 18, 19

Taro, 16, 17, 20

Taylor, J., 9, 23, 24, 65, 66, 78, 180

Taylor, Leahy, and Spinks expedition, 23-25, 78-80

Technology: native technology, pre-colonial, 10, 15, 17, 79, 93; technological change, 8, 28, 78-85, 89-92, 119; Western technology, native attitudes towards, 66-68, 81-85, 88, 96, 116, 123

Tools. *See* Technology

Trade. *See* Economy

Tribe, 36, 39-41, 51, 54, 70; and feasts, 43, 46, 48, 49

United Nations, 27

Vial, L. G., 4, 58-59, 70

Warfare. *See* Fighting

Watson, J. B., 18

Weapons, 19, 57-58, 102

White, P., 14

Widowhood, 19, 33

Willis, I., 1, 23

Witchcraft. *See* Sorcery

Women, 34, 63-64, 90, 92, 119. *See also* Sex roles

Work. *See* Occupations

World War II, effect on Chimbu, 27

Wurm, S. A., 14

For Product Safety Concerns and Information please contact our EU
representative GPSR@taylorandfrancis.com
Taylor & Francis Verlag GmbH, Kaufingerstraße 24, 80331 München, Germany

www.ingramcontent.com/pod-product-compliance
Lightning Source LLC
Chambersburg PA
CBHW050513280326
41932CB00014B/2309